HENRY V's NAVY

HENRY V's NAVY

THE SEA-ROAD TO AGINCOURT AND CONQUEST 1413–1422

IAN FRIEL

The
History
Press

For Colin Richmond

First published 2015

The History Press
The Mill, Brimscombe Port
Stroud, Gloucestershire, GL5 2QG
www.thehistorypress.co.uk

© Ian Friel, 2015

The right of Ian Friel to be identified as the Author
of this work has been asserted in accordance with the
Copyright, Designs and Patents Act 1988.

British Library Cataloguing in Publication Data.
A catalogue record for this book is available from the British Library.

ISBN 978 0 7509 6392 3

Typesetting and origination by The History Press
Printed and bound in Great Britain by TJ International Ltd

CONTENTS

ACKNOWLEDGEMENTS

I would like to offer my grateful thanks to: Serena Cant at Historic England; Gillian Hutchinson for allowing me to reproduce her drawing of the planking of the *Grace Dieu*; Mrs Gill Neal and the archivist, at Wiltshire and Swindon History Centre, for their help in providing images of the '*Holigost* letter'; Anooshka Rawden, Collections Manager, the Society of Antiquaries of London; the staff of The National Archives, Kew; the staff of the Institute of Historical Research, University of London; Sarah Williams of the Museum of London, for her help with images of the Museum's amazing ship's trumpet; John Barlow (Tidal Analyst) and Susan Juggins (Customer Services Analyst) of the UK Hydrographic Office for supplying the invaluable historic tidal data for the eastern end of the Bay of the Seine on three key dates in the years 1415 and 1416.

Anyone writing about Henry V's fleet owes a debt to the work of Dr Susan Rose, who has written extensively about the naval history of Henry's time and of the Middle Ages in general. Susan also produced a valuable edition of the accounts of William Soper for the period 1422–27, translated into English, which will be of great interest for any non-Latinists who wish to see what the sources actually say.

Professor Wendy Childs kindly gave me copies of her transcripts of the Bordeaux customs accounts, an invaluable source for English shipping in the fourteenth and fifteenth centuries. Any conclusions drawn from this data are my own responsibility, however.

My daughter Helen Friel (www.helenfriel.com) has redrawn my map and diagram drafts in this book – not as interesting a job as her usual work in papercuts and illustration, but a huge task and one for which I am very grateful!

ACKNOWLEDGEMENTS

My son, David Friel, has given me a great deal of IT help, including the provision of a laptop when my own went down for the third and last time.

My wife Lynne has supported me during the work on this book in all sorts of ways, including the production of some images. At times it must seem to her that I have been writing this book since the days when Henry V was headline news …

The dedication of this book acknowledges an old debt to a teacher, mentor and friend – and a leading historian of fifteenth-century England.

IMAGE CREDITS

I gratefully acknowledge the following institutions for kindly giving me permission to use the following images: the Trustees of the British Museum: 7; Historic England: 83; Museum of London: 14c; The Society of Antiquaries of London: 1c; The National Archives, Kew (TNA): 20, 23, 5c, 25 and 77; Victoria and Albert Museum: 16c; WSA (Wiltshire & Swindon Archives): 17c and 18c.

Unless otherwise specified, all maps, line drawings and photographs are my own copyright.

NOTES

1. To avoid filling the text with amounts like £166 6s 8d, sums of money are generally rounded up or down to the nearest pound.

2. Late medieval England used the Bordeaux wine tun of 252 gallons as the unit for measuring the carrying capacity of a ship. This was not the same as modern measures of ship tonnage, nor many of those used between the sixteenth century and the present day. Strictly speaking, this text should use the words 'tun' and 'tunnage' rather than 'ton' and 'tonnage'. For the sake of (I hope) greater accessibility, I have opted to use the latter spellings. For those interested in the subject of tonnage measurement, the 1964 paper by F.C. Lane offers a good starting point.[1]

3. Unless otherwise stated, definitions of obscure words are taken from the *Oxford English Dictionary*, via www.oed.com.

4. Dates of birth and death given in the text are taken from the *Oxford Dictionary of National Biography* (via www.oxforddnb.com), unless otherwise stated.

5. Basic data about Henry V's shipmasters and his ships is provided in Appendices 1 and 2, respectively.

6. For information on the careers of fourteenth- and fifteenth-century English soldiers, visit the fascinating database of *The Soldier in Later Medieval England* research project at www.medievalsoldier.org.

7. References to images in the text are given as: (1) and colour plates (1c).

ABBREVIATIONS IN TABLES AND APPENDICES

GS	great ship
S	ship
CA	carrack
BG	barge
BL	balinger
nk	not known

INTRODUCTION

A Thoroughly English Ship

A flock of swans paddled its way among the ships as they cleared the Isle of Wight. A welcome omen, perhaps. Three ships had gone up in smoke just as the force set sail, and maybe the swans drove away the bad luck those pyres portended. A sense of uncertainty and danger must have pervaded the fleet that August day, for Henry V's armada was on its way to invade France.

War creates myths. Whether the swans or the fires were real or just technicolour details added by contemporary chroniclers, we don't know. Swans do swim in the sea, but significantly, a swan also featured on Henry's personal badge. If the swan story sounds a little too convenient, the loss of several ships by fire is easier to believe. With its timber hull, hempen rigging and flammable coating of pitch and tar, a medieval ship was a bonfire awaiting a spark.

The king boarded his 'great ship' *Trinity Royal* on Wednesday 7 August 1415. He had stayed at Portchester Castle on Portsmouth Harbour, and was rowed out to join the huge vessel at its anchorage in the Solent between Portsmouth and Southampton. The *Trinity Royal* was the first of four great ships, each one larger than its predecessor. They were built to impress as well as fight. This duality has been a feature of big warships throughout history, a combination of tactical, strategic and technical requirements and what might crudely be called 'willy waving' by the powerful, once one gets past all the ceremony and symbolism.

The *Trinity Royal* had symbolism aplenty – although not intentionally of the phallic kind, so far as we know – and must have been a stunning sight. The ship's records contain a rich and poetic list of paints and other ingredients used to decorate the *Trinity Royal*, including white lead, red lead, vermilion,

11

copperas, verdigris, varnish, gold, cinnabar, indigo, ochre and tinfoil. This embellishment also extended to the ship's huge canvas sail, which had an embroidered worsted cover bearing the king's arms. The vessel's eighteen flags were heavy with religious symbolism, which reflected Henry's personal devotion to the Holy Trinity, the Virgin and the English saints, St Edward and St George.

The *Trinity Royal's* adornment also featured sculpture. A gilded copper crown sat on an iron spindle in the topcastle, and another golden copper crown rested on the head of a wooden leopard elsewhere on the ship, where the leopard perhaps served as a figurehead. Even the capstan, a utilitarian piece of heavy gear used to raise the anchor, sported a gilded copper sceptre, worked in the form of three *fleurs-de-lis*. The *Trinity Royal* was a thoroughly royal, thoroughly English ship, appropriate for a king who promoted the English language and English patriotism. The three *fleurs-de-lis* on the capstan also featured on the English royal standard, though they were a symbol of French kingship. Their presence on the flags and the *Trinity Royal* represented the claim of English kings to the throne of France. The English fleet was sailing that day to start enforcing Henry's claim.

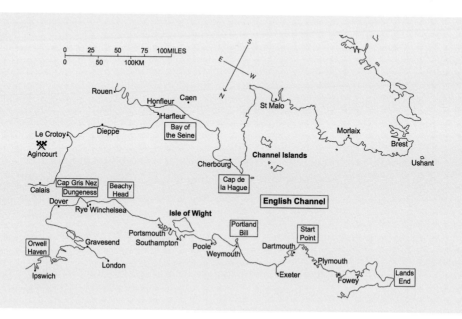

1 The fifteenth-century English Channel from an English viewpoint.

The 1415 invasion led to the capture of the French port of Harfleur, followed by a victory against the odds at Agincourt. That, as things were to prove, was the 'easy bit'. A great deal of blood had already been spilt by the time Henry returned in triumph to London in the autumn of 1415. Much more was to flow in the next seven years, some of it at sea. The king invaded France again in 1417 and went on to conquer Normandy. In 1420, he forced the French ruler to recognise him as his heir, but Henry did not have long to enjoy his success. He died in 1422, and it was his son who would reign briefly as king of an Anglo-French dual monarchy.

Though Henry V's most famous victories were won on land, they were made possible by sea power, by his 'navy'. That navy was made up of the men and ships of the royal fleet and the English merchant marine, as well as many foreign vessels and their crews. This book tells their story.[2]

KINGS, SHIPS AND THE LONG WAR

Henry V and the Hundred Years War

Henry was a complex man, genuinely pious, able, clever, brave, but also utterly ruthless when he had to be. We should judge Henry by the standards of his time, by which measure he was a heroic leader and great soldier. But it should also be remembered that a great many people lost their families, their homes and their lives as a direct result of Henry's march to victory, and for the most part we don't have their perspectives on the king.

Many of Henry's people respected and even idolised him, as far as can be judged. Shakespeare's *Henry V*, although it portrayed a better human being than the real one, caught something of the sense of adoration that Henry inspired in others. As numerous historians have observed, however, Henry V died at just the right time in order to preserve his status as a hero. In the thirty or so years after his death, England lost most of its possessions in France and began a slide towards civil war between aristocratic factions.

So, if Henry's story is ultimately one of failure, why bother to investigate his navy? The first and most important reason is that Henry's fleets made it possible for England to successfully invade France and appear to 'win' the Hundred Years War – however incomplete and temporary that victory proved to be.

The second reason for studying Henry's navy is that it represented something new, in terms of its organisation, strategy and technology. Henry was the first English king to try to keep his experienced royal shipmasters together as a single body – not quite a naval officer corps, but something different from earlier royal fleets. As regards strategy, the seakeeping patrols organised by the Crown were not novel, but their regularity and intensity pointed to a new determination to exert control over the English Channel and English waters. In technological terms, the royal ships were at the proverbial cutting edge, with four of the biggest ships ever seen in England, the rapid adoption of the two-masted rig and England's first ever force of carracks. Fortunately, the royal fleet was well documented, and its records also give us vital information about European ships, cutting-edge or otherwise, that is simply not available elsewhere, even from archaeology.

Finally the dramatic story of Henry's sea war, and of the people who fought it, deserves to be better known. The conflict at sea was fraught with danger for the English, the French and their allies. It is a tale of violence, brutality and folly, as well as one of skill, tenacity and courage.

Henry V's short nine-year reign saw decades' worth of change in politics, war, technology and the ways in which things were done. Love him or hate him, there is a lot to be learned from studying this man and his times.

Henry was born in Monmouth, close to the Welsh border with England, in 1386 or 1387. He was a member of the house of Lancaster, the son of Henry Bolingbroke and great-grandson of Edward III, famous for his spectacular victories over the French. Despite this lineage, Henry might have lived to be no more than a senior aristocrat, but in 1399 his father deposed the king, Richard II (r. 1377–99), and made himself ruler as Henry IV. The young Henry became Prince of Wales soon after.

Henry IV's reign was marked by rebellion in both England and Wales.[3] The prince's early military experience was mainly acquired in the fight against these rebels, particularly in Wales. These conflicts may well have taught the young Henry several hard lessons about the use of the sea in war. The limited application of sea power enabled the resupply of besieged English castles on the Welsh coast but, at the same time, foreign sea power and English naval weakness enabled the French and others to raid the country and land troops in Wales. The use of privateering by both sides also led to rampant piracy, which hit trade and humiliated the monarchy. It is no coincidence that when Henry V dominated the royal council in 1410–11, he made efforts to revive the king's ships as a force.

Henry became king in 1413. He was a man with a deep religious faith, whose devotion to the Holy Trinity was later made manifest in the names and decoration of his four great ships. To Henry and many of his subjects, his victories were proof that God was on his side. The king was also much influenced by history, particularly the example of Edward III. The opening speech at the 1416 English Parliament, which set out the king's thinking, made an explicit link between Edward's victories at Sluys and Poitiers and the recent battle of Agincourt. It was claimed that all three were divine judgements against the French and for the English.[4]

Medieval English government relied on the person of the monarch. He was supported by his royal council and the small-scale machinery of royal administration and justice, but the royal will was what truly mattered. Henry took the business of kingship very seriously; after all, aside from maintaining his earthly reputation and position, in his view, the fate of his immortal soul depended on doing what he saw as the right thing. He tried to ensure stability and peace at home through the law; he aimed to do the same thing in English waters both through legal means and through the exercise of sea power; he did his best to crush threats to the Church, such as Lollardy, and helped to end the Great Schism which had split Roman Catholic Christianity for decades.

In my own opinion, though, people should be careful about hero-worshipping Henry V. It can be easy, when writing military or naval history, to get carried away with the brilliance or ingenuity of leaders, and to forget the people who suffered as a result of these 'geniuses'. There is absolutely no doubt of Henry's personal bravery and skills as a military man, and he was also a capable tactician and strategist. However, this decisive soldier was also a ruthless one. Notoriously, when French reinforcements turned up after the battle of Agincourt had begun, Henry ordered the killing of the French prisoners, to avoid being overwhelmed. Even by the brutal standards of medieval warfare, this was an outrageous thing to do. An even worse act followed during the English siege of Rouen in the winter of 1418–19. In an effort to eke out their dwindling food supplies, the French garrison ejected the poor and those unable to fight. Henry refused to let these refugees through his siege lines, so an unknown number of children, women and men starved to death or died of exposure. John Page, an Englishman who was at the siege, had no doubt of the righteousness of his king's cause, but all the same was haunted by the terrible things he saw: an orphaned toddler begging for bread, a woman cradling a dead child and much more, as all the while death silently took the innocent victims of a 'complex' man.[5]

The Hundred Years War and the English Fleet

At the time, no one thought of it as 'the Hundred Years War'. The phrase was invented in the nineteenth century to link together a series of Anglo-French conflicts that were fought between 1337 and 1453. England's long association with the land mass that is modern France dated back to the Norman Conquest. Although the English Crown lost Normandy to the French in 1204, it retained the duchy of Aquitaine (essentially Gascony) in south-western France until 1453.

Edward III (r. 1327–77) was the first English king to try to make himself king of France. He had a dynastic claim to the French throne, and though the Anglo-French war that broke out in 1337 was not at first ostensibly about this, from 1340 Edward included 'King of France' among his titles. Most of the actual military combat in the different phases of the Hundred Years War took place in France, Gascony or Flanders. The English inflicted extraordinary levels of death and destruction on France, and won famous victories at the naval battle of Sluys (1340) and the land battles of Crécy (1346) and Poitiers (1356). In 1347, Edward III was able to capture Calais, a valuable gateway to the Continent which the English held until 1558. The fighting only touched English soil directly when the French and their allies raided the English coast, or when they intervened via Scotland or Wales.

The war was far from continuous, and between 1369 and 1415, things went pretty much the way of the French. However, the English claim to the throne occupied by the Valois family remained a potentially powerful *casus belli* for any king who wanted to use it. Henry V was that man: the intermittent madness of the French Valois king, Charles VI, and vicious infighting among the French aristocracy, gave him his opportunity (see plates 2 and 3).

Henry's victories in France led to the 1420 Treaty of Troyes that saw him and his descendants recognised as the heirs of Charles VI. Henry's young son Henry VI was later crowned king of a dual Anglo-French monarchy, but as an adult he proved to be a failure as a ruler. The war in France continued. Eventually, the English were driven out of Normandy in 1450, and three years later they lost Gascony.

Sea power was essential to the English in the Hundred Years War. The English merchant fleet was pressed into service on innumerable occasions to fight, to carry armies and to make raids, and did so with success. Merciless coastal raiding was one of the worst aspects of the sea war, and it was perpetrated by both sides (see plates 2c and 3c). The effects and the memory of it could linger for a long time. In 1421, the town of Rottingdean in Sussex asked for a reduction in its tax assessment because of depopulation that followed flooding and a French raid. The raid had taken place forty-four years before.[6]

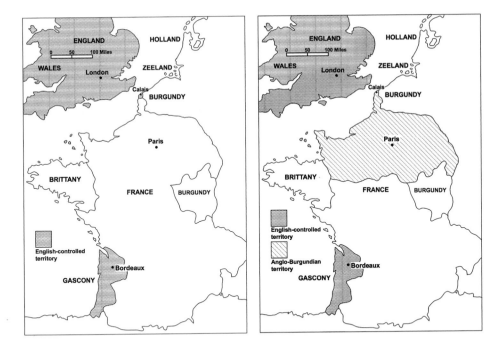

2 (Left) England, France and Burgundy 1413.

3 (Right) England, France and Burgundy 1429: seven years after Henry V's death, most of northern France was under the control of England or Burgundy; by the end of 1453, the only part of mainland France still in English hands was Calais.

The King's Ships 1399–1413

The reign of Henry IV is not known for its naval history, but it was not a peaceful time at sea. Between 1401 and 1406, the Glyndŵr rebellion in Wales received naval support from first the Scots, then the Bretons and French, and there were attacks on ports in Devon (see plate 4). In 1405, a French invasion force landed in Milford Haven to help the Welsh rebels, and in February 1406, the French effectively blockaded the mouth of the Thames.

Despite such incidents, Henry IV, the French and others seem to have pursued a kind of proxy war through privateering, largely avoiding direct conflict. Privateering was a system whereby the Crown licensed seafarers to attack the shipping of hostile nations. The trouble was that privateering easily turned into indiscriminate piracy. Medieval English monarchs faced a real problem when it came to dealing with piracy, because they had to rely on the shipping of the kingdom to support their naval expeditions and wars, and the best sea fighters were often also the best pirates. One incident illustrates this dilemma perfectly. In 1406, the master of a Plymouth barge and his crew were arrested on a clear charge of sea robbery. However, they were let go on the grounds the barge was 'needed at present to resist the malice of [the king's] enemies at sea'. It was not quite a 'get out of jail free card', because the master was told to present himself at court at a later date, but it was not far from it.[7]

4 The watergate of the fourteenth-century fortification that protected Dartmouth harbour. Dartmouth was attacked by the Bretons in 1404, but they were driven off.

The king's ships were vessels owned directly by the Crown, but they were never very numerous in Henry IV's time. He started his reign in November 1399 with three royal ships, though within a year this had grown to six. The royal fleet remained at five or six units until 1407, when it began to decline. By November 1409, it had dwindled to just two ships, a river barge and a decrepit big ship, the *Trinity*, that was languishing in dock. The fleet was revived briefly in 1410–11, when Prince Henry held the reins of power in the king's council, but declined again after he lost his influence. By the time Henry V came to the throne in March 1413, only four vessels were left, two of them non-operational.[8]

5 Aerial view of the Tower of London.

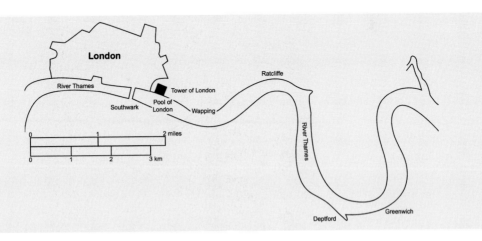

6 London and Greenwich in the early fifteenth century.

In the early fifteenth century, the names of English royal ships carried the suffix 'of the Tower', meaning the 'of the Tower of London', a sense akin to the later 'HMS'. This associated them with the principal royal castle and arsenal, where their gear was stored, but probably also described their normal mooring place, close to the Tower in the Pool of London. Further downriver, there were a number of simple mud docks at Greenwich used to lay up the royal ships over the winter, to help preserve them from stormy weather (see plates 5 and 6).

The largest ship in Henry IV's fleet was the 300-ton *Trinity*, built for Richard II. It was described as a 'great ship' in at least one source, and was quite possibly one of the biggest ships in the country. Henry IV owned a total of about seventeen or eighteen vessels during his reign – eight or nine ships, one carrack, seven balingers or barges and one galley. The galley, the *Jesus Maria*, was one of three due to be built in 1412. The vessels were meant to be used to convey the ailing Henry IV to the Holy Land, where, it was prophesied, he would die. Mortality overtook the project, and Henry expired in the Jerusalem Chamber at Westminster Abbey instead. The huge and expensive *Jesus Maria* was completed, but ended up as a derelict on the Thames.[9]

The king's ships were not a state navy in the modern sense. They were, quite literally, the personal possessions of the sovereign. This meant that while fighting was part of their 'remit', they were used for all sorts of other purposes. In Henry IV's reign this included the transport of wine and VIPs: despite the desperate and dangerous events at sea in his time, the royal ships only took part in a handful of war operations. This reality – that the monarch was both the overall naval war commander and the 'first shipowner' in the land – would not begin to change until the Tudor period. The 'royal navy' of Henry IV and Henry V was not the same as the modern Royal Navy.

Late medieval England may not have had a state navy, but it did have admirals. Until 1408, English admirals were normally appointed for no more than a year, usually in nominal command of the shipping on the east coast, or the south and west coasts (see plate 7). The first Admiral of England (with national responsibilities) was created in 1408, when the Earl of Dorset (later Duke of Exeter), took up the post. He served until 1426, but the role of Admiral was as much a legal one as a military one, and the Admiral seldom functioned as a fleet commander in Henry V's reign.[10]

7 Bronze seal matrix of Richard Clitherowe, Admiral of the West, 1406 (the name is also spelled Clederowe or Cliderowe). Clitherowe was a royal official, merchant and shipowner, one of two men appointed as temporary admirals at the urging of merchants, in an unsuccessful attempt to police English waters.[11] Clitherowe later played a key role in hiring hundreds of Dutch ships to support Henry V's campaigns. (British Museum)

2

THE NAVY OF ENGLAND

Use the word 'navy' nowadays, and most people will assume that you're talking about a state navy of some kind, such as the British Royal Navy or the US Navy, or perhaps a mercantile marine like the Merchant Navy. Neither usage fully expresses what fifteenth-century English people meant by the 'navy' of their country.

The word 'navy' migrated from Norman French into Middle English, its meaning changing over time, and was current in English documents in the late 1300s, by which time it denoted 'a group of ships'. The problem is, those who used the word were not always talking about the same group of ships. In October 1416, shipowners complained in Parliament that lack of tonnage payment for ships arrested by the Crown was ruining them and destroying the 'navy' of the realm, which they owned. In other words, they were equating the trading fleet with the 'navy' of England – the 'merchant navy', in effect. At other times, 'navy' referred to all the shipping of England, both the trading fleet and the royal ships, as in a call to arms made in 1419. In writing about 'Henry V's Navy', I am using the term in its broadest medieval sense, to mean 'the fleet of vessels that served the realm' – and, therefore, also served the king. The ships deployed by Henry comprised the royal ships, the vessels of his subjects and hired foreign ships.[12]

England and the Sea Trade of Europe[13]

England and Wales are maritime nations, with large seaboards relative to their land area, and in the late Middle Ages they had at least 192 ports between them. This figure, however, does not include the many small and middling river ports that also existed and enabled sea trade to penetrate deep inland, especially in England. Unfortunately, Wales does not feature greatly in the maritime history of Henry V's reign. Its trade was badly damaged by the long years of the Welsh revolt in the early 1400s, and even before that date, the coastal towns mostly operated within a pattern set by English trade and political control.

England's geographical position put it astride the most important shipping routes of northern Europe. Vessels from northern and southern Europe mainly passed through the English Channel, and England lay just across the North Sea from the Low Countries, one of the industrial and commercial powerhouses of Europe. A good geographical position was not the same as having a strong trading economy, however.

8 Significant ports of medieval England and Wales.

9 The great harbour at Dartmouth.

Late medieval England was a second-rate economic power, and that may be putting it generously. In Henry V's time, England's major exports were all raw materials: grain, Cornish tin and wool. The cloth industry was growing, but this manufactured product would not overtake wool as an export until the 1430s. The situation was not helped by the fact that the English merchant community lacked the organisation and sophistication of major competitors like the Italians and the Hanse. As a result, some significant sectors of the country's overseas trade were dominated by foreign merchants and their shipping.

Despite such difficulties, English vessels of the period were to be found carrying all kinds of goods, including wool to the Low Countries, salt from France and dried cod (stockfish) from Iceland. The one really important bulk trade under English control was the import of wine from Gascony. Gascony had belonged to the English Crown since the twelfth century, a link that benefitted English merchants, created a need for larger ships and familiarised English seafarers with the challenges of navigating a long and sometimes very dangerous route. For all that, the combination of the weakness of English overseas commerce and the other factors above meant that by Henry V's time, English sea power was at a low ebb.

10 Late medieval English sea trade.

11 Town walls at the former West Hithe, Southampton. The defences of the port were improved after a devastating French raid in 1338, and here they even incorporated the remains of earlier houses.

12 The imposing Wool House, Southampton, early fifteenth century. Built as a secure store and weigh house for wool, it underlines the importance of the commodity in England's overseas trade.

Arrested Development: The English Shipping Industry

The rather glib phrase 'English merchant fleet' will be used in this book as a handy catch-all term for the non-royal shipping of the kingdom. Aside from its uses in war, this fleet had four main functions: to carry cargo and passengers, to fish and to rob other people's ships. There was nothing especially 'English' about this, and the description would probably fit other European shipping industries of the period just as well.

There are no available figures for the overall size of the English merchant fleet before the reign of Elizabeth I, but it is possible to identify changing trends over time. The surviving Bordeaux customs returns are a useful guide to the state of England's merchant fleet, and they paint a rather stark picture for the early 1400s.[14]

English ships were measured in terms of the number of Bordeaux wine tuns or tons that they could carry. It is reasonable to assume that most ships taking on wine at Bordeaux loaded as much as they could safely transport, so the port's records give a pretty good idea of the approximate maximum tonnages of vessels involved in the trade. The fourteenth-century Bordeaux accounts show that a century before Henry V's time, the English merchant fleet included a much higher proportion of ships of 100-plus tons than was the case in the first decade or so of the 1400s. The surviving early fifteenth-century data is scrappy, but consistent. It all comes from roughly the same months in the extant years (October/November to February–April), and for each period the number of English and Welsh ships recorded is almost the same:

English/Welsh ships' cargoes:	1402–03	1409–10	1412–13
0–49 tons	78	58	57
50–99 tons	65	66	56
100–149 tons	4	18	21
150–199 tons	–	2	5
Total nos	**147**	**144**	**139**
Total tons loaded	**7199**	**9366**	**9276**
Largest single cargo (tons)	**125.5**	**189.5**	**185**

Incomplete as it is, the information all points towards one conclusion: England was short of big ships in the early 1400s. If they had existed, they would have featured on the country's main bulk-trade route in larger numbers. Even in the 1412–13 period, only 15 per cent of the ships calling at Bordeaux were able to load 100 tons or more, and just a handful of these could take more than 150 tons. This was not just a 'blip': the next set of surviving Bordeaux customs returns, from 1431, shows a fleet with not very many more big ships, though there was a recovery later, in the 1430s and 1440s.

The greatest English ports in the early 1400s were London, Bristol and Hull, though there were other significant harbours, such as Fowey, Dartmouth, Southampton, King's Lynn and Newcastle. The ports were home to merchant communities, but perhaps because of the organisational weaknesses of English trade, there is little sign of complex shipowning partnerships in England in this period. Typically, ships belonged to just one or two people, such as shipmasters and merchants, though the aristocracy also sometimes also owned vessels. This pattern of ownership may have put serious limits on the capital available for building and operating ships.[15]

Just how much medieval English kings knew or cared about the state of the country's merchant fleet is open to question, though there is good reason to think that Henry V feared that the country was short of shipping, because he hired so many foreign vessels. He certainly knew about the significance of shipping for international trade, because merchants moaned in Parliament about the threats it faced, and the king tried to deal with the piracy that damaged trade and the merchant fleet. Henry's interest in the merchant fleet was not just economic though, because the nation's 'navy' was also a resource for war.

Historian Craig Lambert has identified a number of ways in which the Crown obtained ships for war service in the fourteenth century, most of which were still used in Henry's time. Aside from acquiring his own ships, or arresting merchantmen, the monarch could call on the limited and archaic feudal ship service provided by the Cinque Ports. The king could also offer tax breaks to private owners in return for ships; he could hire English and foreign vessels;

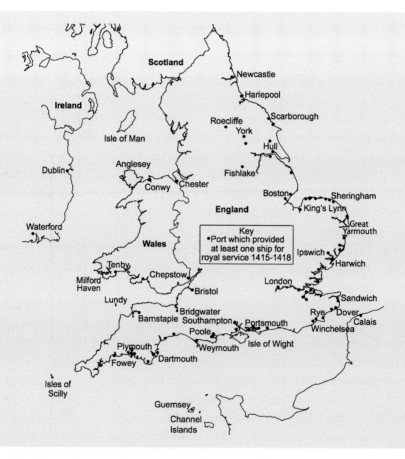

13 English ports known to have contributed ships to royal fleets, 1415–18, including inland settlements. The sources are not complete, and the true number of ports with ships involved in war service may have been much higher.

he could acquire forfeited vessels or enemy prize ships; groups of towns could be induced to provide or build ships, and pardons could offered to masters and crews in return for sea service. Henry's personal fleet came from a variety of sources, including construction, purchase, forfeit, capture and gift (see Appendix 2). Many of the foreign vessels he used were hired, but the vast majority of non-royal English ships in his service were conscripted or 'arrested'.

Shipping arrests for royal service were often imposed with little or no warning, and must have been a nightmare for anyone engaged in sea trade. The process generally began with an order to arrest all ships and other vessels above a certain size in a given range of ports. Their masters and crews would be ordered to take them to a certain place by a specific date, ready to be mustered and to set sail on a particular operation. Local officials sometimes arrested vessels, but the orders were normally carried out by a king's sergeant-at-arms, a military officer. The sergeant-at-arms was usually accompanied by a clerk to record the details of ships and masters.

It is not always clear how the officials ensured that arrested vessels and crews went where they were told to go, though sanctions could be applied to those who disobeyed. Violating a royal order could lead to outlawry, prison and other unpleasant legal consequences, and this may have been enough for most shipowners and masters. Sometimes shipmasters were required to deposit a sum of money with the authorities as surety before they left for the assembly port. Occasionally, more direct measures were used. In early 1417, a group of arrested ships sailing from London to Southampton were accompanied by two royal balingers, the *George* and the *Gabriel Harfleur*, 'driving' them like sheepdogs with a flock of sheep.

Shipowners certainly complained about arrests, and Henry V gave them a lot to grumble about. In the eight years between July 1414 and June 1422, the government issued at least twenty-seven arrest orders. Some of these were very localised, as when Dover and the other Cinque Ports were told in 1414 to provide 'passagers' (small cross-Channel ferries) and other vessels to transport English ambassadors to Calais, along with their retinues of men and 500 horses. At the other end of the scale were the 'nationwide' arrests. In practice, these generally applied only to the ports on the south-west, south and east coasts between Bristol and Newcastle upon Tyne. No attempts seem to have been made to extend the dragnet to Welsh ports, and the orders seldom touched north-west England, although the county of Lancashire was included in 1417. These large-scale seizures were used for major expeditions, such as big seakeeping voyages and the two invasions of France.

The Crown made efforts to pay the crews it conscripted, to help prevent desertion and to ensure that the men could eat: half-starved sailors were not of much use on a war voyage. The shipowners themselves were given a payment called 'tontight'. This was paid at a rate of 3s 4d per ship's ton for every three months in royal service. Formalised in 1380, it was meant to cover wear and tear, though in Henry's reign there were recurrent complaints that it was not being paid.

Most of the English ships used by the Crown served as transports, taking soldiers, horses and supplies to France. Some ships were also used to move cargo between English possessions in Normandy, like the *Thomas* of London in 1417, which spent several weeks carrying victuals from Harfleur to Caen, in company with a small London balinger named *John* and a vessel from Hastings.

The complete fleet lists for Henry's two invasions have not survived, unfortunately. The names of over 200 English and Dutch vessels from the 1417 invasion fleet are known, however. This is because they were granted licences allowing them to go home in September 1417, and copies of these survive. It is very unlikely that these ships represented the whole of the transport fleet, but they do give some sense of the types and origins of the merchant ships that had been arrested. None of the licences give tonnages, but most specify the type of vessel involved. The English ships came from places as far apart as Bridgwater in Somerset and Newcastle upon Tyne; in addition, there was also one crayer from Tenby in Wales, another from Calais and two Gascon balingers. The breakdown of the 117 English types is as follows:

Type	Number
Balinger	8
Barge	2
Collet	1
Crayer	53
Dogger	5
Farcost	20
Lodeship	10
Passager	1
Picard	5
Scaff	1
Ship	9
Spinas	1
Unknown	1

14 Reconstruction of a small late medieval ship, Southampton. Not much bigger than an open boat, this one-master probably typifies some of the small English vessels used in Henry's invasion fleets.

Two things in particular stand out about this group. The first is that most of the vessels were very small. Crayers seldom exceeded 100 tons and often had a carrying capacity of less than 50 tons. Farcosts seem to have been of roughly similar size, as were doggers, which were fishing boats. The others were almost all tiny craft of one kind or another, which suggests that the arrests had scooped up almost anything that would float (the minimum tonnage limit was set very low, at 20 tons). Secondly, the geographical scope of the arrests was very wide, taking in vessels from the usual coastal ports as well as places deep inland that otherwise never supplied craft for royal service. Fishlake and Roecliffe in Yorkshire, for instance, stand on rivers that connect to the Humber, but they are a very long way from the sea (see plate 13). Notwithstanding this, each supplied a boat that helped Henry to invade Normandy.

It very much looks as if Henry's officials were scraping the bottom of England's sea-power 'barrel' in 1417. This ties in with evidence of serious deficiencies in the number and size of vessels in the English merchant fleet. These deficiencies were made up, to some small degree, by vessels from

English-held Gascony, but they were not enough. In order to invade France and fight his naval war, Henry needed foreign shipping.[16] One of the main reasons for the lack of English ships, I believe, was a lack of English sailors.

The English Seafaring Population

In the years 1348–50, the Black Death swept across Asia and Europe and killed between one person in three and one in two. There are no accurate national population statistics for this period, but estimates based on a range of indicators suggest that before the great plague, there were between 3.5 and 6 million people living in England. By 1400, that had fallen to 2 or 3 million, and the population may still have been falling in Henry's time. There are no signs of a rise until around the mid-fifteenth century. This catastrophic drop was due both to the Black Death and to the succession of national and local plagues that followed, which prevented any recovery.[17] Disease scythed through seafaring communities as much as the rest of society, and Susan Rose has suggested that this may have created difficulties in recruiting men

15 Mid-fourteenth-century graffiti on a wall in the church of St Mary, Ashwell, Hertfordshire, recording visitations of the plague.

to serve in the king's ships in the second half of the fourteenth centu. Henry V's time, there is evidence that England was suffering from a ser. shortage of sailors.

This was not the case in the years immediately before the Black Death, when Edward III was able to raise medieval England's biggest war fleets (the biggest, at least, that can be reliably documented). In 1346, he invaded France with a force of some 700 English ships and thirty-eight foreign vessels. The English crews comprised just over 14,000 men; those of the foreign ships 1,000 or so. English-operated fleets could still muster 14,000 crewmen in the 1370s, though it isn't clear how many of these sailors were actually English.[18]

According to contemporary sources, Henry V led an invasion fleet of 1,500–1,600 ships to France in 1415, twice the size of the fleets of the 1340s. How was this possible in a world with many fewer people? The problem here is that these figures derive from chronicles and not from the original records of the fleet. The latter would have given an accurate count of ships, but unfortunately they haven't survived and medieval chroniclers were often unreliable when it came to 'big numbers'. As Anne Curry has demonstrated, chroniclers' estimates for the size of the armies at Agincourt range between 6,000 and 100,000. She also shows that English sources tended to exaggerate the size of the French army, making the glory of the English victory all the greater.[19]

The figure of 1,500 or so ships is very unlikely to be true, unless someone double-counted by reckoning each ship's boat as a separate vessel. As we have seen, the available indicators suggest that England's national fleet was smaller in number and tonnage than it had been in the fourteenth century. To a large extent, the paucity of English shipping was made up by foreign vessels. The fleet that sailed to France in 1415 contained hundreds of hired Dutch ships, and the 1417 invasion fleet was much the same. There was nothing new about using foreign ships in royal expeditions, but even in the huge 1346 fleet, foreign participation stood at no more than 5–6 per cent of the total force. Hiring large numbers of vessels from abroad was expensive and problematic: it is very difficult to believe that Henry V would have used this option on the scale that he did, unless he already knew that England could not supply his shipping needs by itself.[20] Besides the scale of the foreign hirings, there is another indicator of the weakness of the English shipping industry, to be found in the pay records of Henry's own ships.

The pay structure of royal ships was very simple. Masters were paid 6*d* per day, ordinary sailors received 3*d* per day and boys got 1½*d*. The sailors

received an additional payment of 6*d* per week, called a
ward', perhaps intended to encourage men not to jump ship.
an additional officer in some vessels, the 'constable', a junior
fficer, probably employed to help organise the crew to fight. Like
.er, he was paid 6*d* per day.

ages of ships' boys or 'pages' are not known for this period, though
a their pay rate, they cannot have been regarded as possessing the full
ength and capabilities of an adult. Whatever the precise functions of boys
aboard ship, as servants or assistants to cooks and so on, one would not
expect to find more than, say, two or three in a crew of thirty. Evidence from
1439–51 supports this, with English crew lists showing an average of only
two or so boys per ship. This was certainly not the case in the early years of
Henry's reign.

The pay accounts for 1413–16 record forty-eight voyages made by royal
vessels, forty-one of these by sailing ships and seven by oared balingers (see
plate 56). Proportions of boys in the balinger crews were low, presumably
because effective rowing relied on the muscle power of grown men. The
sailing ship crews were quite different. On thirty-four of the sailing ship
voyages (83 per cent), boys made up at least a quarter of the crew. In half of
these cases, the proportion of boys was one-third or more. Many of these
were trading/convoy operations – on offensive war operations, the number
of boys stayed the same and the number of adult mariners increased.

This phenomenon, almost a 'boys' fleet', affected ships of all sizes. When
the 500-ton *Trinity Royal* carried Henry V to Normandy in 1415, over one in
six of its 200-strong crew was a boy. At the other end of the scale, the 70-ton
Margaret went to Gascony in 1416 with nine adult seafarers and six boys.
The 220-ton *Cog John* made two Bordeaux voyages for the Crown: on both
occasions, it carried twenty boys in a crew of forty-four. One wonders how
many of these young lads escaped the ship's wreck on the Breton coast in 1414.

The king's government possessed wide-ranging powers of conscription
and seafarers could be compelled to serve in royal ships. Even with these
powers, it was not able to find enough adult sailors to crew ships, and the
balance was being made up with youngsters. This points to a real crisis in
seafaring manpower. Though we don't have many detailed crew records after
1416, there are signs that the predicament was still affecting the royal fleet
in 1420. By then, officials could not find enough people – men or boys – to
crew the great ships properly.[21] It was little wonder that Henry ended up
hiring so many foreign ships and their crews.

Foreign Ships

Obtaining foreign ships for war service was neither easy nor cheap because it involved diplomacy, whose wheels had to be greased with cash and concessions. Henry negotiated with John the Fearless, Duke of Burgundy, to ensure that Burgundy did not get in the way of his plans to invade France. However, Burgundy was also allied to the Duke of Holland, ruler of Holland and Zeeland, and by getting the complicity of Duke John, Henry gained access to the large Dutch shipping fleet. At the end of February 1415, two royal servants, Richard Clitherowe and Reginald Curteis, were detailed to go on a mission to the Duke of Holland and others in the Low Countries.

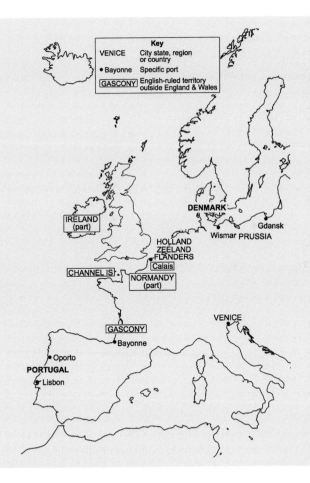

16 The origins of foreign ships used by Henry V, 1415–19.

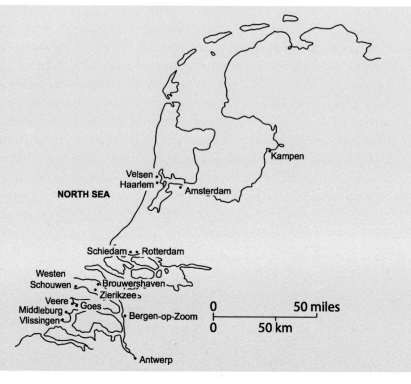

Kampen

Velsen
Haarlem
Amsterdam

NORTH SEA

Schiedam • • Rotterdam

Westen
Schouwen
Brouwershaven
Zierikzee
Veere Goes
Middleburg
Vlissingen
Bergen-op-Zoom

0
0
50 miles
50 km

Antwerp

17 Ports in the Low Countries known to have contributed vessels to Henry V's fleets, 1415–17.

The aim was to hire Dutch ships to take part in the forthcoming invasion of France, though their final commission was not issued until 4 April 1415. The men took £2,000 with them on their initial visit to the Low Countries. As Ian Mortimer suggests, this huge sum must have been a down payment for future services – services that had been negotiated in advance.

The initial plan was for the Dutch ships to come to London, Sandwich and Winchelsea, though some probably later went on to join the vessels also being mustered in the Solent. One contemporary report claimed that 700 ships from Holland were due to arrive in England that summer, though the true figure may have been much lower. A Venetian courier who had been in Bruges until 18 June said that 125 cogs and 181 other ships, both large and small, had been recruited by Henry in the Low Countries. This figure of 306 ships does sound more credible, because it gives a rough breakdown of the fleet in terms of types.[22]

Richard Clitherowe was despatched to the Netherlands again in 1417 to hire ships, this time for the second invasion of Normandy. As in 1415, we cannot be too sure of the total numbers hired, but in September 1417, 116 ships from the Low Countries were allowed to depart from Normandy, at the same time as the 117 English ships discussed above. Seventy per cent of these Dutch craft came from just five ports: Goes (26), Haarlem (21), Rotterdam (13), Dordrecht (13) and Middleburg (11). Most came from Holland and Zeeland, though there were also three from Antwerp in Flanders.

Eighty per cent of these vessels (93) were described as 'cogships', with ten crayers, eight 'ships' and a few minor types. We don't have tonnage figures for most of these vessels, but surviving payment details for ten of the cogships describe ships that had a capacity of between 30 and 50 tons, with tiny crews of five or six. To take one 1417 example, John Jacobson was master of the 46-ton cogship *St Jacobesknyght* of Bergen-op-Zoom in the southern Netherlands. His crew consisted of four men and one boy, which must have

18 Ship on the seal of Amsterdam, *c.* 1400, which could well have been described as a 'cogship' (after Ewe, 1972, no. 3).

been close to the bare minimum number of sailors needed for a one-master. Jacobson signed on for English service at London on 21 February 1417, and had to sail to Southampton by 15 March to join the invasion fleet. He served right through the summer and his ship was one of those allowed to quit Normandy on 1 September.[23]

A small number of large foreign vessels were used as warships in seakeeping patrols, though it is not always clear if they were hired or arrested for service. Five Prussian ships, with a total tonnage of 1,600 tons, may have been in the fleet that went to the battle of Harfleur in 1416; in 1417, three Gdansk vessels and a Dutch ship, all between 170 and 400 tons, were used in seakeeping patrols.[24] Small foreign warships could be useful, too. Henry V acquired the temporary services of three Portuguese galleys, commanded by Sir John (João) Vasques, to patrol 'the waters of the Seine' during the siege of Rouen in 1418–19, apparently through the good offices of his ally João I, King of Portugal.[25]

The most controversial foreign ships used by Henry's forces came from Venice. The Venetians traded routinely with northern Europe in galleys and carracks. It was a valuable trade for them, and the members of the Venetian Senate were horrified when they heard, in late April 1417, that the English had seized three of their *coche*, or carracks, for use in the fleet that Henry was

19 Inside the Venetian Arsenal. Though the Arsenal has been much rebuilt over the centuries, this photograph gives some sense of the size of the great dockyard that produced the Venetian carracks seized by Henry V.

gathering against the French. Unlike their Genoese rivals, who served the French as seagoing mercenaries, the Venetians wanted no part in the Anglo-French conflict. They could not do much about it, however, beyond making protests, and Henry ignored those.

The three carracks belonged to Marco Giustinian, Pietro Landro and others, and were under the command of Giovanni Bono de Ziliolo, Marco Bocheta and Antonio Ungareno. The English referred to them as the *St Louis*, *St Marie* and *St Jacob*, and the closest they could get to Bono's name was 'Jon Bon'. At least two of the carracks served in the seakeeping patrols of 1417, and they may have taken part in the great battle of that year. Bono's vessel was 'devastated' in one operation, and he received an old sail and sail bonnet from one of the captured Genoese carracks in recompense.

The three ships were still under English orders in early 1419, because they joined a sea patrol in January and February that year, helping to defend the Isle of Wight against a feared attack by carracks. The three vessels carried 380 sailors and men-at-arms between them, and the government supplied them with victuals, beer and firewood. By 1419, the patron of the *St Louis* was Jacopo di Otranto, and the vessel had a crew of sixty-one; its tonnage (worked out on the basis of tontight payments) was 500 tons, making it of similar proportions to the captured Genoese carracks that were already in English hands.

Although it appears they were conscripted into Henry's war, the crews of the Venetian carracks seem to have accepted their lot, because it would have been easy enough just to sail home. Ungareno's carrack was later captured by the Genoese, some time before the Anglo-Genoese truce of June 1421. The details are confused, because the ship was taken into Dartmouth, and that is only likely to have happened after the truce. Ungareno petitioned the royal council for redress. A group of Italians was appointed to assess the level of compensation due, but he may never have got his money.[26]

Clerks, Cash and Carracks: The King's Ships

The royal ships were not a navy in the modern sense, but under Henry V they had important warlike functions. They often acted as the core of war fleets, despite almost always being outnumbered in major operations by arrested and hired ships. The composition of the royal fleet underlined the weaknesses of the English shipping industry, because at least one-third of the forty-six major vessels were foreign-built (see Appendix 2):

Origin	Great ship	Carrack	Ship	Balinger/barge	Totals
England	4	–	–	8	12
Brittany★	–	–	3	3	6
Genoa	–	8	–	–	8
Spain★	–	–	3	–	3
Not known	–	–	10	7	17
Totals	**4**	**8**	**16**	**18**	**46**

★known or presumed. The non-operational galley *Jesus Maria* and four unused Breton crayers are not included.

Three men administered the king's ships between 1413 and 1422, William Catton, Robert Berd and William Soper. Catton was a career royal servant, and was clerk of the king's ships from 1413 to 1420, but also served as a Sussex town bailiff and Member of Parliament. Robert Berd managed the construction of the massive *Grace Dieu* at Southampton as clerk of works, and also seems to have been a career official – there is no evidence that he was a shipwright. Soper came from a different background. He had important mercantile interests at Southampton, and belonged to the coterie of merchants and craftsmen who ran the town and its port. His association with the royal ships stretched over nearly thirty years, and he served as keeper of the king's ships from 1420 to 1442.[27]

These officials bore heavy responsibilities. Huge amounts of royal money went through their hands, and they had charge of a great number of expensive ships and their equipment. The clerks of the king's ships often paid the crews, too. Income and expenditure needed to be documented down to the last farthing and the ship and store inventories had to record the acquisition and disposal of even the most trivial pieces of gear. All of this work was carried out using Roman numerals and an exchequer board to add up or subtract the figures, and the results were set down in huge parchment rolls. Their accounts are mainly written in terse, abbreviated Latin shot through with Middle English and foreign words for different pieces of equipment. They are long documents: Catton's 1416–20 account runs to over 44,000 words. Detailed analysis of the accounts suggests that they were accurate and faithful records. To take just one minor example, an iron grapnel supplied for the galley *Jesus Maria* in 1411 was still in the store, and still listed, a decade after the galley itself became a waterlogged hulk. These accounts are key documents, for they tell us how the royal vessels were equipped, and often how they were used.

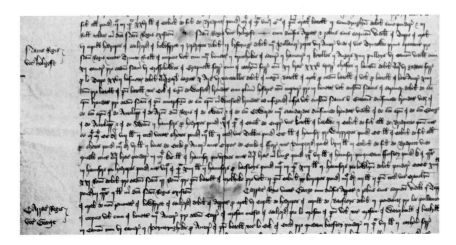

20 A extract from the enrolled accounts of William Soper, 1420–22. This section includes inventories of gear in the great ship *Holy Ghost* and the carrack *George*. (TNA E101/49/29, m 8, The National Archives, Kew)

Much of the technical information about ships in this book derives from these records. Given the disparate sources of the royal ships, there is reason to think they were not unrepresentative of the general run of shipping in north European waters at the time.[28]

The accuracy of the accounts is all the more extraordinary because very few people were employed in the administration of the ships, usually just the clerk and a couple of purveyors, who helped to keep the accounts but also travelled around England purchasing supplies and materials. Despite this remarkably lean bureaucracy, the system worked. These otherwise prosaic accounts are monuments to the hard and detailed work of the sober, serious people who kept the royal fleet in being.[29]

Income and Outcome

Navies have always been expensive, and medieval English kings were often short of money. These two facts, as much as the presence or absence of war, help to explain why English royal fleets of the Middle Ages waxed and waned over time. For example, the great royal navy built up by Edward III (r. 1327–77) in the early part of his reign was in real decline by the 1370s, apparently due to a lack of money in the royal coffers and perhaps a shortage of seafarers.[30]

Most of the funding for the king's ships came from the royal Exchequer in London and derived from taxes and customs dues, though from 1416 the scale of operations meant that some crew wages were channelled through officials other than the clerk of the king's ships.[31] Alongside the money from the Exchequer, the clerks brought in some income for the king's ships by selling surplus materials. Significant amounts of direct funding also came from freight rates levied when the royal ships carried cargoes for merchants. This can be followed closely for 1413–16, in which period the royal ships earned a total of £2,055, equivalent to just over a quarter of Catton's total expenditure. The ships seem to have been acting as convoy escorts on these journeys as well as cargo vessels, a very useful way of offsetting some of the costs of the voyages. The king's ships of Henry's time also received important income in kind, in the form of some ten prize ships and their contents captured in Henry's time.[32]

The money paid out by all three officials gives some sense of the sheer extent of the operations of the royal fleet:

Expenditure by Period

1413–16:	£7,808 (24.5%)	
1416–20:	£17,472 (54.9%)	
1420–22:	£6,557 (20.6%)	
Total:	**£31,837**[33]	

In modern terms, the total outlay only equates to just over £22 million, but such simple equivalents don't do justice to the scale of the medieval expenditure. An ordinary sailor of the time would have needed to spend the entire reign at sea in order to earn just 0.001 per cent of the sum lavished on the royal ships.

These figures only relate to money spent by officials directly concerned with the king's ships; they do not include, for example, the wages paid for the two invasion fleets and some other major operations. However, they do reflect the relative levels of naval activity, 1416–20 standing out as the most intensive period. Just over one-third of the £31,837 (approximately £11,200), went on the construction and maintenance of four vessels, the great ships. These were the true 'capital ships' of their day and the 1,400-ton Grace Dieu alone cost around £3,800 to build and equip. As it turned out, this was pretty much money down the drain, though the performance of the other three great ships in battle seems to have justified their enormous cost (see chapters 7 and 8).[34]

Catton's first account (1413–16) separates the crew wage payments from the maintenance expenditure. This makes it possible to work out what proportion of each ship's service period was taken up with voyages, and how much it cost to maintain over that time (see Appendix 3). The figures show that fourteen of the nineteen vessels were on voyages for more than 50 per cent of the time (this included any periods spent in ports other than the port of origin). The average daily 'maintenance spend' for ten of the vessels ranged from less than 1s to 4s per day. This was irrespective of the total time each of these vessels was in royal hands, its size or the number of days it was engaged in voyages. A few were more expensive, however: the average spend for the 220-ton *Cog John* was high, at 10s per day at sea; for two of the balingers it was 12s each.

It is clear that Catton was spending the maintenance money effectively, because the majority of the ships were operational for between half and two-thirds of their total service time. The relatively consistent nature of the maintenance costs also points to work being carried out in a planned and timely manner, another sign of good management. This was also something of an achievement, because there were no royal dockyards to maintain these highly perishable ships and the work relied entirely on an artisanal shipbuilding industry. Unfortunately, the 1416–22 accounts don't generally separate crew wages and maintenance costs, so it's not possible to work out exactly how much time the ships spent at sea in that period. It is apparent, however, that the majority of the royal fleet was kept in an operational state in the very dangerous years of 1416 and 1417.

William Catton retired from his post in February 1420. Soper took charge of the royal ships as keeper, and stayed in harness until 1442. Catton went on to do a third spell as an MP in 1421, and became a country gentleman. He died in 1431.[35] William Soper also prospered; like Catton, he eventually joined the gentry, dying in 1459. Robert Berd remained in royal service until at least 1422, but nothing more seems to be known about him, a rather sad fate for a man who managed the construction of the *Grace Dieu*, the greatest ship England had ever seen.[36]

The Functions of Henry V's Ships

Although Henry's fleet was not a proto-Royal Navy, the range of functions it performed under the pressure of war was in some ways not too different from that of the British navy in the twentieth century. The table below gives a brief summary of the main tasks of Henry's fleet:

	Great ship	Carrack	Ship	Balingers/barges
War patrol	★	★	★	★
Expeditions and/or invasions	★		★	★
Port defence/area defence		+		+
Sea trade/convoy		+	★	+
Fishery protection				+
Transport of war supplies			+?	+
Reconnaissance/secret missions				★
Transport of VIPs	★		+	★
Miscellaneous			+	+

★ major function
+ minor function

The only activity that stands out as being really unusual for a modern navy is the important one of 'sea trade'. However, as I have suggested, the trading voyages probably had a dual purpose: to earn money from freight charges, and to help protect English merchantmen.

The table above makes clear just how versatile the balingers and barges were, and, conversely, the degree to which the great ships were war vessels first and last. Even including them in the 'transport of VIPs' function is overstating things a little, because these VIP voyages involved taking Henry V and his brother the Duke of Bedford on war operations. The carracks, those that proved seaworthy, were either used in sea patrols or, later, on trading voyages, apart from the carrack *George*'s temporary function as a guard ship in the River Hamble. The 'miscellaneous' column covers voyages of an administrative nature, such as the ship *Grand Marie*'s taking pay to the Calais garrison in 1414 and the balinger *Swan*'s delivery of letters to the king in Normandy in 1418.[37]

3

SHIPMEN AND SOLDIERS

The Seafaring Community

'Shipman' was a Middle English word for 'sailor'. Not a lot is known about the ordinary sailors and ships' boys of Henry's time, though it's apparent that places like Dartmouth and many of the Cinque Ports were true 'sea towns', where shipping, sea trade and fishing were the primary industries and the majority of men naturally gravitated to working at sea. A recent study by Marianne Kowaleski points out some features of later maritime communities that were probably also common to medieval ones: men away from home for long periods on voyages, a high death rate at work, and port communities in which women played a bigger role in running households than was common in inland settlements. Sailors and their families, it almost goes without saying, were mostly poor. In Henry's day, the 3d a day pay of a sailor was less than that of the lowest grade of shipwright. Shipwrights and other artisans normally worked for six days a week, with Sundays off; at sea, the sailor had to work seven days a week in a job that could easily cost a man his life.[38]

The crews who manned Henry's royal ships were not specialised 'naval' sailors in any sense, but came from the same manpower pool that supplied the merchant and fishing fleets. We can't discover much about these people as individuals, though the names of some of them do survive in the handful of extant muster lists from Henry's reign. One set, apparently compiled for seven ships on the same voyage, relates to the royal carracks *Andrew* and *Christopher*, the ship *Grand Marie*, the balingers *James* and *Swan* and two Dartmouth vessels, the *Grace Dieu* and *Nicholas*. There is also a separate muster list for the balinger *Gabriel Harfleur* during the time that Andrew Godfray was master (c. 1417–22).[39]

21 Sailors and trumpeters on the seal of Dover, c. 1300 (after Nicolas 1847, p.386). Although this image predates Henry V's time by 100 years, the shipboard work it depicts – hauling on a cable, climbing up to the sailyard and trumpeting a ship's departure – would have been very familiar to sailors and ships' boys of the early 1400s.

22 Oarsmen, after a manuscript of *c.* 1470–72 (Nicholas 1847 after British Library Harleian MS 4379). The hard work of rowing was a job for adult sailors.

The crew lists for the seven ships date from between August 1417, when the two carracks were captured, and the summer of 1420, when the *Andrew* sank (see plate 23). The documents show 390 men and boys aboard these ships, plus the names of twenty-three men who were not mustered – an absentee rate of 5.5 per cent, a low figure, given the lack of an organised press gang. For once, the number of boys or pages was quite small, twenty-six out of 390 (6.66 per cent).

Taking the eight ship musters together (including that of the *Gabriel Harfleur*), the majority of the 430 men present had English surnames, such as Atwell, Atwick, Brown, Clerk, Cook, Monk, London, Smyth, Stoner, Taplow and West. Roughly one in eight shared a surname with at least one other shipmate, suggesting possible family links. The family connection is made quite clear in some cases by shared rare surnames or something more explicit. For instance, the master of the carrack *Christopher*, William Tenderley, had a John Tenderley in his crew, and a John Browne also shipped aboard with a John Browne 'junior'. Likewise, John, Thomas and William Taplow in the *Gabriel Harfleur* were surely related.

Only around one in twelve of the surnames appears to have been of non-English origin, including five Welshmen (Boyce, Bryce, Davy and Pryce), a couple of Gascons, some Spaniards, a Venetian and others. These crew lists only offer us a small sample of Henry's crews, but they do not suggest that ships in the king's service made great use of foreign manpower, despite the evidence for the shortage of English sailors.

23 Muster list of the royal carrack *Christopher*, *c.* 1417–20. (TNA E101/55/12, m 2, The National Archives, Kew)

The Royal Shipmasters

Henry V employed around sixty-one men as shipmasters during his reign. Like the ordinary sailors they led, they must have started out their seafaring lives in trade, fishing or piracy. Whilst the records aren't complete enough to reconstruct anything like their full biographies, it is possible to explore the lives of a small number (see Appendix 1 for a summary).

At an initial rate of 6d a day in royal service, shipmasters were not particularly well paid, considering the responsibilities and dangers of their job. The relative impecunity of shipmasters and the poverty of most sailors goes a long way to explaining the high incidence of piracy in the Middle Ages. However, if shipmasters were successful as traders or sea fighters, they could become quite rich. William Richeman, master of the carrack *George*, was described in 1425 as a 'gentleman and yeoman'.[40] None of Henry's shipmasters became national figures – the world of Drake and Hawkins was a long way off – though most survived war service and outlived the king.

The sailor with the longest record of employment under Henry V was John William. A 1419 document described him as being 'of Kingswear' (on the east side of Dartmouth harbour), though his roots may have been Welsh. He worked for the Hawleys of Dartmouth in Henry IV's reign, in charge of their balinger *Craccher* (the future royal vessel), and committed at least one sea robbery. William entered royal service in August 1413 and commanded three royal ships, the *Rodcogge*, *Cog John* and the innovative 1,000-ton *Jesus*. He also co-owned the small ship *Margaret* with the king, one of two royal shipmasters (the other was Richard Rowe), to have a half share in a royal ship.

William and the *Jesus* probably took part in the Earl of Huntingdon's 1417 battle off the Chef de Caux; shortly after, he transported Henry V across the Channel for his second invasion of France. William was one of the royal shipmasters granted a retainer in 1417 of 10 marks per year (£6 13s 4d), which was doubled in 1419. He went into sea trade after Henry V's death, and may have become a prominent Southampton citizen, perhaps living into the mid-1400s.[41]

Richard Rowe was another man with a long record of service, ranging from 1416 to the mid-1430s or later. He probably grew up in Greenwich. A Richard Rowe (his father?), owned land in the Deptford area in the late 1300s and 'Richard Rowe, mariner of Greenwich', was involved in property dealings in Deptford in 1415 and 1416. Rowe only commanded balingers in royal service, the *Swan* (20 tons) and the *Valentine* (100 tons). He served at the siege of Rouen and in other operations, though in the mid-1420s he was still owed £95 for crew wages paid on these voyages. Like a number of the other royal balinger masters, he was implicated in robbery at sea, and was arrested at one point by William Catton. After a spell as a prisoner of the French in the 1420s, Rowe returned to royal service in the mid-1430s as master of the rebuilt balinger *Little Jesus*.[42]

It is likely that all of Henry's shipmasters had blood on their hands, for combat was an inescapable part of medieval seafaring. Chaucer's portrayal of his Shipman character, quite possibly modelled on John Hawley the Elder of Dartmouth, underlines this. The Shipman is described as a man of great professional knowledge and skill, but also a ruthless killer who drowned captured crews.[43] Given the brutal seaborne world they inhabited, there is a certain irony in the fact that one of the royal shipmasters was wanted for a murder committed on land. William Cheke served Henry from 1417 to 1422, but was put in custody at Plymouth in 1419 for a killing. He escaped his gaolers either through cunning or bribery, and never seems to have answered for this alleged crime. Henry's shipmasters were probably rather dangerous people: if there had ever been a job description for the post, 'a propensity for violence' would have been listed as an essential personality trait.[44]

Professional Skills

Whatever their personal qualities or behaviour, there is little doubt about the abilities of Henry's shipmasters as sailors and fighters. Although some ships were wrecked in harbour, only three or four royal vessels were lost at sea between 1413 and 1422 and just one was captured (see Appendix 2). What may have helped here was that these men were mostly operating in familiar waters, their own 'backyard' – the North Sea, the English Channel and the route to Gascony (see plate 56 and Appendix 1). Four future royal shipmasters – John William, Robert Shadde, Hankyn Pytman and John Piers – were all at Bordeaux in October 1412, as masters of wine ships, and they were not alone in having pre-war experience of this difficult journey. Like a modern London taxi driver 'doing the knowledge', most masters probably learned routes and the nature of different havens by heart and by hard experience.

Seafarers needed only a small range of navigational instruments to help them put this knowledge into practice. There is no evidence that English sailors used charts at this time, but certain navigational tools are found again and again in the inventories of Henry V's ships. These were sounding leads and lines, magnetic compasses and sandglasses. Sounding leads measured water depth and, with a lump of tallow stuck in a recess at the base, could be used to bring up seabed samples. The nature of the seabed under his keel could tell a sailor roughly where he was, and of course knowledge of the water depth was essential for safe sailing.

The magnetic compass, sometimes described as a 'sail needle', revealed the direction of magnetic north. The 32-point compass card was known by the late fourteenth century, and was vital when setting courses. Some ships also had binnacles, a special fixed structure to house and protect the compass – the binnacle in the *Trinity Royal* was covered with lead.

The sandglass or hourglass, called a *dioll* ('dial') in Middle English, made it possible to mark the passage of time. This meant that a master could time the crew's watches aboard ship, or measure the time spent sailing in a particular direction. Distances at sea were not known accurately in miles, but there is evidence that English sailors in the fifteenth century thought in terms of 'kennings', a measure that represented the distance from shore that the summit of a 100ft hill could be sighted from the top of a 50ft mast. In practice, the kenning equated to about 20 miles.[45]

Two other items of navigational equipment deserve a mention: lanterns and *fanes*. Lanterns were ubiquitous, either in the form of 'great lanterns' to mark out a ship at night or smaller kind needed for work below decks and in cabins. *Fanes* or wind vanes were less common in the inventories of Henry's ships, but were listed in a few. These were streamer-like flags flown at the masthead in order to show the direction of the wind. They could be large: the carrack *George* had two, one 18 yards in length, the other of 4 yards (16.5 and 3.7m respectively).

Medieval vessels must have run watch systems, to allow one part of the crew to rest while the other worked, but very little is known about this. Sandglasses may have served to time these, but the only direct evidence of a watch system in Henry V's ships comes in the inventory of the ship *Thomas*, which had a brass bell, *pro vigilacione marinariorum*, 'for the watch[es] of the sailors'.[46]

Masters and Men

There was no code of naval discipline for Henry's ships, so it's reasonable to assume that long-established sea laws like the Law of Oléron and its offshoots applied to shipboard life. These laws recognised the right of the master to run his ship, but also respected certain traditional rights of sailors regarding issues such as pay, food, care and discipline. For instance, if a master struck one of his crew, the man had to endure it without striking back, but if there was a second blow, the man could defend himself.[47] The fact that Henry's fleet functioned as well as it did suggests that in most cases masters and men established a viable working relationship. Certainly, apart from the Earl of Devon's 1420 seakeeping voyage, there is no sign of mutinies. This is all the more surprising because there is no real evidence that the royal shipmasters had any junior officers to help them, apart from the occasional constable. The master's responsibilities were huge, and it is likely that running a royal ship was an exceptionally pressured and lonely existence.

Salaries, Shipmen and 'Balinger Men'

In 1417, Henry V put his most valued shipmasters on annual salaries. The idea was not without precedent, but it was implemented on an unprecedented scale and put these men on a higher level than their contemporaries. The men in charge of the larger vessels, like William Payn of the carrack *Paul* or Jordan Brownyng of the great ship *Holy Ghost*, were granted 10 marks per year (£6 13s 4d) and masters of smaller sailing ships like the *Grand Marie* were paid £5. The balinger and barge masters received 5 marks apiece (£3 6s 8d). Nicholas Rodger describes these men as perhaps 'the first corps of regular sea officers'.

The first set of nineteen salary grants came on 12 August 1417, less than three weeks after the Earl of Huntingdon's victory off the Chef de Caux. The grants clearly represented an intention to reward good service and to keep a proven and successful group of commanders together. It was not the beginning of the 'royal navy' as we know it, because almost all of these men left royal service after Henry's death in 1422. It was, however, a sign that Henry V saw his royal fleet as something more than a temporary wartime expedient.[48]

But a shipmaster did not just command *any* type of vessel, at least not in Henry's service. Out of the sixty-one shipmasters, only three – William Cheke, Ralph Huskard and Robert Shadde – commanded both royal sailing ships and oared vessels. Otherwise, there was a sharp division between 'sailing ship men' and 'balinger men' (see Appendix 1). This was also reflected in their differential salary rates. The two types of vessel were rigged in much the same way, so this cannot have been the thing that set them apart. Part of the explanation may have been that the command and co-ordination of a rowing crew required specific skills not possessed by all shipmasters. Balinger crews could be quite big, and this was not a job for a second-rate master, but for all that, the balinger commanders got lower salaries.

Aside from any technical issues, the reasons behind this very real difference between 'sail and oar' may have been social. It's possible that balingers and the people who crewed them were seen as tainted in some way by the balinger's association with piracy, though sailing ships were also used to commit piratical acts. Perhaps more importantly, sailing ships bore the brunt of the hand-to-hand combat in battle, while balingers tended to fight in a supporting role. Balingers also stood lower in the water than sailing vessels, possibly reinforcing ideas of inferiority. Medieval military ideology was shot through with notions of honour, and it may be that the shape and tactical uses of balingers simply made them seem somehow less 'honourable'.

Life on Board

Life aboard a sailing warship at this time would seem awful to most modern people. Overcrowding was the norm. On a three-month seakeeping patrol in 1417, the *Little Trinity* carried ninety-two sailors and soldiers, with just a few hundred square metres of deck or hold area in which to move. They had to share this area with several months' worth of victuals, the armour and weaponry of the soldiers, as well as the hull structure, rig, cables and other gear. Within this space, the crew had to sail the ship, and both soldiers and sailors needed to be ready to fight. All of this in a long deployment in which few set foot on dry land! Splitting the crew into watches would have eased the pressure on space by staggering sleep periods, but perhaps not by much.

It's likely that conditions in balingers and barges were even worse. Oared vessels had to be low-built, meaning there was probably no more than a single deck, with little space underneath. For example, in 1418 the balinger *Anne* crammed 100 sailors into a narrow hull that cannot have exceeded 98ft (30m) in length. Tent-like structures could be erected over the deck to provide some shelter in harbour, but life in a balinger must have been remarkably harsh.

It is anyone's guess as to how cooking and mealtimes were organised in Henry V's ships. Tableware does not feature in most ship inventories, so those on board must have brought their own, or a commander supplied it. When Lord Morley's ship was being made ready to lead arrested vessels from London to Southampton in 1416, items purchased included wooden cups, bowls, dishes and platters, probably for use by the ordinary crewmembers. Pewter plates, saucers, chargers, ewers and other metalware were also bought, no doubt destined for Morley's table.

The standard diet of ships' crews did include fresh food when it was available, but for long voyages it was necessary to use preserved food. This meant salted fish, beef, mutton or pork, or dried cod, called stockfish, which was imported from Iceland. Fresh bread might be available when a ship was in port, but the most common form of bread eaten by sailors was biscuit, a hard-baked concoction of flour and water. Eating a ship's biscuit was probably a bit like trying to get your teeth around a ceramic floor tile, though in practice a lot of biscuit may have been stewed along with salt fish or meat. The normal drink aboard ship was beer, which would last longer than water because it was boiled during the brewing process, and also supplied additional calories.

Victuals acquired for Morley's ship included fifty quarters of wheat flour (for baking bread or biscuit), a pound's (£1) worth of fresh loaves, as well as beef and mutton, a large amount of salt, salt fish, stockfish and butter, and around 16,000 pints of beer. In addition to this, there were provisions probably intended only for the Lord and his senior officers: red and white wine, some Malmsey, venison, chickens, haddock, mackerel, salmon, lampreys, plaice and 'one great dogfish'. The food was cooked in a well-equipped kitchen which boasted a large 24-gallon (109 litre) iron-bound brass cauldron, eight smaller brass cauldrons, iron hooks for suspending pots over the cooking fire, a griddle and even an iron hammer for softening stockfish. Unfortunately, we don't know how big Morley's crew was, or even the ship's name, but the vessel seems to have been well supplied. Sailors need to be adequately fed, otherwise they cannot work properly, and this may have been one of the attractions of sea service for poor men. If there had been any serious deficiencies in the food supply for Henry V's ships, one would expect to find evidence of mutinies over the issue, and there is none.

As well as feeding crews, ships needed to be able to get rid of their waste. The medieval sources are generally silent on this aspect of war at sea, but most of Henry's ships had an enigmatic piece of equipment called a *sketfate*. Primly described as something 'to serve in times of necessity' in one contemporary document, the Middle English word is more brutally descriptive: it means 'shit vat'.[49]

Making a Statement: Inside the Minds of Sailors and the King

Ships' crews were not just concerned with the strictly practical issues of trading, fishing and fighting. They also took religion and ideology to sea, because religious belief and observance permeated society and politics in medieval Europe. Henry V's piety was perhaps a bit more sophisticated than that of the average sailor or peasant, but he shared the widespread view that the supernatural played a part in all aspects of life. Concomitant with this was a belief in the power of prayer and votive offerings to move God, the Trinity, the Virgin Mary and the saints to come to the aid of an individual, a cause or even a kingdom.

The names of most medieval ships had a clear votive purpose, like offerings at a shrine. A ship was named after the Trinity, Jesus, the Virgin or a saint as a way of offering those in the ship, and the ship itself, a measure of divine protection. Evidence of this can be found in almost any list of medieval European vessels. For example, the 117 named English merchant ships involved in the 1417 invasion had just twenty-eight names between them. All bar three were clear religious dedications, with the Virgin Mary far and away the most popular, gracing thirty-two vessels (27 per cent). Most of the vessels in the royal fleet carried religiously inspired names. Almost all of Henry V's ships were named after aspects of the divine, the four biggest – *Trinity Royal*, *Holy Ghost*, *Jesus* and *Grace Dieu* – representing the Trinity or facets of it and reflecting Henry's personal devotion (see Appendix 2).[50]

Interestingly, there doesn't seem to have been any superstition about renaming ships. The old Spanish ship *Santa Clara* was reborn as the *Holy Ghost*, and all of the carracks captured in 1416 and 1417 were renamed. Some ships had dual names: the ship *Rodcogge* was previously called the *Flaward* (possibly *Flavard*) of Guérande (southern Brittany), though even four years after coming into royal service it was still occasionally referred to as *Flaward*.[51]

Only a handful of ships in Henry's fleet had non-religious names. The oddest was that of the balinger *Craccher*, given to the king by the Dartmouth shipowner and pirate John Hawley the Younger in 1416. At first sight, it seems to be the French verb *cracher*, 'to spit', a visceral act of aggression and piratical contempt. However, Middle English also had a verb *cracche*, meaning 'to grab' or 'snatch'. If the balinger really was called *Snatcher*, it was an apt choice for a vessel owned by Hawley.[52]

In the royal ships, ideology was not just confined to names or the specifically religious sphere. In essence, the monarch was also the state in medieval England, anointed by God, and this made patriotism something rather more than a matter of waving flags. Patriotic symbolism featured heavily in some ships, in the form of heraldic lions or leopards and the French *fleur-de-lis* of the king's arms, or with the flags of the English saints George and Edward, which flew from the big ships *Nicholas* and *Katherine* as they sailed to Normandy in 1415. Henry believed in the divine right of kings, and proclaimed his autocratic views in a startling way on the great ship *Holy Ghost*. It carried the French motto, *une sanz pluis*, 'one and no more'. As Ian Mortimer has shown, the words came from a French version of Homer's *Iliad* and asserted that no one but the king should be master.[53]

As well as sporting particular heraldry, it's likely that the hulls of royal ships were also painted, a common practice in Henry IV's reign. There are only a few direct references to this from Henry V's time, however. A Southampton painter named John Rendyng was employed to paint the topcastle, stern and sail of the balinger *Anne* in 1416 for 10s. Two other named craftsmen worked on the *Holy Ghost* when it was being built at Southampton. These were Robert Brown, a carver who was paid £4 13s 4d for making the wooden antelope and another heraldic device (*signum*). This was a substantial amount of money, but William Stone, who painted the ship, was paid a great deal more – £20.[54] Some ships also carried pavises, wooden shields placed on the sides of the hull and castles and used as a defence against arrows. To judge from medieval pictures, they were often painted with heraldic devices (see plate 26). Only a minority of the royal ships had pavises listed in their inventories, though the storehouses for the royal fleet kept large numbers in stock.[55]

24 South door of St Saviour's church, Dartmouth. Although the door bears the date 1631, the magnificent iron lions rampant are thought to be fifteenth century, and closely resemble those found in the contemporary English royal arms that featured on some ships' flags.

Pirates and Privateers

The men who manned Henry V's ships were drawn from a maritime world in which violence was commonplace. Nicholas Rodger describes the medieval sea as a zone beyond the boundaries of civilisation, and there is a lot of truth in this. Piracy itself was not made a felony in England until the sixteenth century, and the distinction between acceptable and intolerable action at sea was sometimes a 'grey area'.

The situation was complicated by the 'right of reprisal'. It was widely understood that if foreign sailors robbed a ship and goods, and the owners or master could not get satisfaction in the foreign courts, they could apply to the English government for a licence to attack ships of that nation until they had recouped the value of their losses. This medieval version of 'restorative justice' was of course deeply flawed and dangerous, and could lead to a spiral of mounting criminality, with licences abused as a handy figleaf to cover villainy.[56]

Murder was also a part of piracy. If nothing else, to some sailors it made a certain brutal, tactical sense to kill captured crews, and men could signal 'death without quarter and war to the knife' by flying a red flag as they swooped into attack. However, the violence of pirates and privateers was not completely without restraint. For example, sea trade was only seriously interrupted when piracy approached the level of a sea war, as it did in Henry IV's reign. Also, the many complaints made by *survivors* of sea robberies suggest that piracy and massacre did not always go hand in hand.

There are also instances that show the extent to which sea robbery was a business, and not always a murderous business, at that. It was common to ransom potentially valuable captives, though at times ransom demands could exceed the ability of victims' families to pay them. In some cases, English and foreign sailors worked out local deals between themselves, presumably to limit both bankruptcy and killings. In 1412, the mariners of Lydd and Romney in Kent had a local treaty, sealed by religious oaths, with the seamen of the Harfleur area in Normandy, which set an agreed tariff for ransom demands. At around the same time, sailors in Devon and Cornwall had a mutual agreement with Spanish seafarers that men from captured ships were allowed to take passage home, apparently without paying ransom.[57]

Medieval piracy was an endemic disease that at times assumed epidemic proportions. Henry IV had effectively encouraged it by encouraging privateering. His son tried to reduce piracy with certain measures such as the 1414 Statute of Truces. The problem for all medieval English governments was that the pirates were often the same seafarers they turned to in times of war. In some places, too, pirates *were* the local authorities, like the father and son named John Hawley (Elder *c.* 1350–1408; Younger *c.* 1384–1436), who were based in Dartmouth. Both enjoyed a long series of public appointments (mayoralties and membership of Parliament), both were merchants and shipowners, both served the Crown in war and both profited from decades of sea robbery.

Harry Pay of Poole (d. 1419) was another dangerous man. Known as 'arripay' to the Spanish, he attacked so much Spanish shipping that when the Castilians raided the English coast in 1406, they made a special point of ravaging Poole. It was not at all unknown for pirates like Pay to drag England into conflict with other countries, but for all that he was employed in officially sanctioned actions against French shipping 1405 and 1406 and seems to have ended up the water bailiff at Calais, a plum appointment in such a busy port.[58] Many men of this kind, both masters and mariners, must have sailed in the ships used by Henry V. Their experience qualified them as sailors and as fighters, but when it came to piracy, a lot of them were probably part of the problem, not the solution.

War by Contract: Soldiers aboard Ship

In the absence of a standing army, medieval kings raised military forces from the aristocracy, gentry and others in return for pay. It was war by contract. The same system was used to supply soldiers for sea service, as many military indentures show. Plate 25 shows an agreement made in 1415 between two men, John Clifford and Robert Rudyngton, and the king. They were to supply forty men-at-arms and eighty archers to serve at sea for fifty days.

25 War by contract: an agreement between the king, John Clifford and Robert Rudyngton to serve at sea with soldiers, 18 February 1415. (TNA E101/70/1/812, The National Archives, Kew)

26 Men-at-arms in a ship bound for war. The crush of figures is unrealistic, but reflects the very real overcrowding in war vessels. The shields on the ship are pavises, which served both as heraldic devices and as protection against projectiles. (Nicholas 1847 after British Library Harleian MS 4379)

The men-at-arms received the usual rate, 12*d* each per day, and the archers 6*d* per day. The contract set few other specific conditions, beyond limiting stopovers on English-controlled coastlines to a night and day, and prohibiting the capture of merchant ships without orders.[59]

The shipmaster does not seem to have been part of the normal chain of command for embarked soldiers. The soldiers were often grouped in traditional military units of twenty men called *vingtaines*. They were hired by a particular commander, and a ship's military complement served under one or two captains. These soldiers were not 'marines' in any sense, but ordinary soldiers assigned to go to sea, and it's likely that each war voyage with troops began with massive outbreaks of seasickness.[60]

Men-at-arms were armoured foot soldiers who carried swords, lances and other hand weapons (see plates 26, 27 and 28). They would resemble the traditional image of a 'knight' to modern audiences, though it was possible for men from humbler backgrounds to serve as men-at-arms, alongside members of the aristocracy and gentry. Archers were drawn from society at large, and tended to have little armour – merely a helmet and perhaps a reinforced jacket called a *jakke* (see plate 47).[61]

The general ratio of men-at-arms to archers embarked on a ship at this time was one man-at-arms to two archers. This was markedly different from the ratio used in the Agincourt land campaign, of 1:3. The reason for this

27 Brass of John Wantele (d. 1424), St Michael's, Amberley, West Sussex. Wantele wears the armour and sword of a man-at-arms, with a surcoat emblazoned with three lions' heads, perhaps the symbol of the Morley family.

28 Side view of a tomb effigy of *c.* 1400, Dorchester Abbey, Oxfordshire. The head-to-toe armour of a man-at-arms was well shaped and relatively light, though the chain mail shown on this figure was falling out of favour by Henry V's time.[62]

difference may have been that it was thought impractical to carry large numbers of archers aboard ship, as Anne Curry suggests. Naval battles generally ended with boarding actions. The lightly armed archers and their bows would have been of less use in this phase of an action than men-at-arms with their armour and hand weapons. However, whilst the ratio might be observed at the level of a fleet, the actual distribution of the two types of soldier between ships could vary a great deal.[63]

War Crews

The fighting power of a royal warship did not just rely on soldiers. Most royal ships had their own weaponry, hand weapons and sometimes cannon and armour. This equipment was there to be used by the sailors, because the men-at-arms and archers brought their own gear with them. The sailors were probably commanded in battle by a constable, though these officers were not carried in all circumstances and it's likely the master often took on this role.

Vessels sailing on war expeditions received additional sailors, to help both work the ship and fight in action. For example, seven royal ships used on offensive operations in 1415 were crewed by complements that were between just over one-quarter to two-thirds larger than the crews they carried on trading and convoy escort voyages. The ship *Grand Marie* received nineteen men in addition to its usual twenty-eight crew, for instance, and the small balinger *Paul* packed in ten extra mariners alongside its normal twenty-four oarsmen.[64] Most of these ships also had significant numbers of boys aboard, but the additional crew always comprised adult sailors.

The Perks of War – Prize Ships and Goods

Throughout the history of war at sea under sail, the primary objective was seldom to destroy the enemy's ships and their contents, because these things had a market value as prize goods. Documents of Henry V's time describe these as 'the perquisites of war' – a 'perk' of putting your life on the line.

The value of captured ships and merchandise is shown in an account submitted by Sir Thomas Carew for his 1417 seakeeping expedition.[65] The prize rules meant that a quarter of everything captured, or at least a quarter of its value, belonged to the king. The Castilian Spanish were by now the enemies of England, and Carew's force captured five Spanish ships. Four of the Spanish ships seem to have been captured together. In accordance with the prize rules, one of the four ships, along with its cargo of iron, wool and other goods, was given to the Crown and became a king's ship. It was known as the *Christopher Spain* in its brief and unremarkable career in English royal service. The fifth Spanish vessel was captured in the harbour of Saint-Valéry-en-Caux in Normandy, about 16 miles south-west of Dieppe. Its crew tried to scuttle the vessel, causing so much damage that Carew had to spend £20 on repairs just to make it seaworthy enough to get to Southampton.

The king got one quarter of the proceeds of the ship when it was sold, but he also had to stump up one quarter of the cost of repairs.

The *Christopher Spain* was one of at least ten vessels that were taken by seakeeping patrols between 1415 and 1417 and then joined the royal fleet (see Appendix 2), not counting the carracks taken in battle. If the rule of 'one quarter to the king' was observed by the patrol leaders, this means that these patrols took forty or more prizes, a valuable haul for those in charge and their crews.

4

SHIPS OF THE WOOD AGE

Medieval England belonged to the 'Wood Age', a period that stretched from prehistory to the Industrial Revolution. Almost everything in daily life – hearth fires, housebuilding, transport, tables, everyday platters and spoons – relied on wood in some way.[66]

Medieval English ships were mostly built of oak timbers and boards. Tough, slow-growing and durable, oak is ideal for shipbuilding, and English woodlands had a lot of it. The records of the Henry's ships are full of references to oak, and to planks called 'Englishboard' that almost certainly derived from oak woods. For instance, building the 1,400-ton *Grace Dieu* at Southampton swallowed up over 2,735 oaks, most from the king's New Forest. The only other significant shipbuilding material was beech – the *Grace Dieu* also used

29 The spreading English oak, mainstay of medieval English shipbuilding …

30 … and as a shipwright might have seen it.

up over 1,100 beech trees. How it was used is not very clear, although at least one fifteenth-century shipwreck proved to have a beechwood keel. The Crown could draw on massive reserves of free timber from the royal forests, though timber supply may have been more of a problem for the ordinary shipbuilder.

Shipwrights looked for two types of timber: good, straight pieces for keels and beams, and the 'compass timber' that could be made into frames and other curved or angled hull parts. Boards were made either by using an axe to cleave a trunk in long, radial splits (you could make up to sixteen boards in this way), or by sawing. Some good-quality oak timber and readymade boards called 'wainscot' were also imported from the Baltic, along with fir and pine.

Until the mid-fifteenth century, the typical north European ship was clinker built. The hull was made from of a shell of planks, which was the main load-bearing component. This was built first, with a few frames inserted to help maintain shape, though other frames and beams went in as the hull progressed.

The planks overlapped and were fastened together at their edges by nails driven in from the outside. The nail points went through metal washers called roves, on the inside of the hull, and they were then secured by being hammered down across the roves. This process was called 'clenching', and gave its name to the nails and the construction method. There was just one skin of planks in most ships, so far as we know, but Henry V's giant 1,400-ton *Grace Dieu* had three layers of planking in each colossal strake or run of boards (see plate 33).

31 The end of a cloven board from Henry V's *Grace Dieu*.

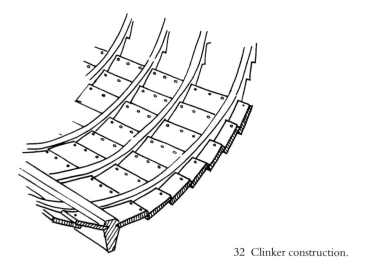

32 Clinker construction.

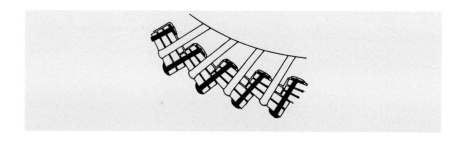

33 Cross section of the triple-skin clinker planking of the *Grace Dieu*, with clenchnails and roves represented in black and trenails in white. (Gillian Hutchinson)

Shipbuilding was not a high-status craft in medieval England. Few people have heard of John Hoggekyn, for instance, yet this man built and almost certainly designed one of the biggest ships in medieval Europe – the *Grace Dieu*. Hoggekyn was eventually granted a royal pension of 4*d* a day because 'in labouring long' about the royal ships 'he is much shaken and deteriorated in body'. This was a rare show of gratitude to a talented and hard-working artisan, but in terms of social position Hoggekyn ranked below the masons and artists who worked on churches and royal palaces. This was despite the fact that, unlike the great buildings, his creations had to go to sea and fight.

The structure of the north European shipbuilding trade had evolved out of clinker technology. In England, the workers, their functions and typical pay rates were as follows:

Worker	Daily pay	Functions and responsibilities
Master shipwright	8*d*	manager, designer, financially accountable
Boarders	6*d*	(probably) shaping timbers and boards, supervising clenchers and holders
Clenchers	5*d*	worked inside the hull, clenching nail points over roves
Holders	4*d*	worked outside the hull, holding in the nails as they were clenched

It seems that shipwrights were actually rather thin on the ground in late medieval England. Even a busy port like Southampton could not supply enough shipwrights to work on Henry V's giant *Grace Dieu*, so attempts were made to conscript craftsmen from the West Country. Men who resisted were jailed.

Like timber, most of the other materials that went into a medieval ship were also organic. The gaps between the planks were caulked using old rope, animal hair or moss. The caulking and planks were waterproofed with pitch and tar (imported from the Baltic) and finished off with a coat of tallow, manufactured from animal fat. The cordage – the ropes and cables – was made of hemp, as was the sail canvas. The canvas all came from overseas, because none was made in England. The country did manufacture its own ropes and cables, at places like Bridport in Dorset and Kings Lynn in Norfolk, though some imports were also used. Vessels of the time had an insatiable appetite for cordage, since even tarred natural fibres could rot.

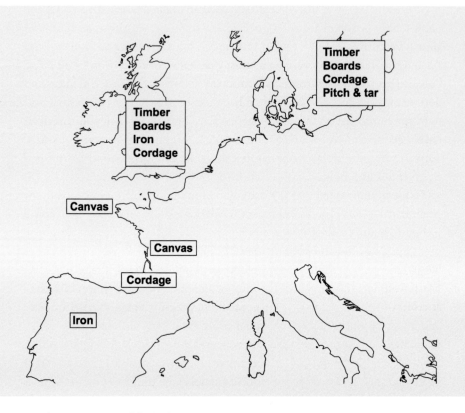

34 The main sources of shipbuilding materials used in fifteenth-century England.

The only significant inorganic shipbuilding material was iron, which came either from English sources or from Spain. The Spanish variety was regarded as better, but it was more expensive. Clinker technology did use cheap wooden nails (trenails) in large numbers, but it also relied on the expensive two-part clenchnail and rove. A pound (0.45 kg) of clenchnails bought for the 120-ton royal balinger *Anne* in 1416 cost 1½*d*, nearly half a day's pay for a shipwright holder who worked with them. Many other types of iron nails, spikes and bolts were also used, and the *Anne* went to sea with over 6 tonnes of iron in its hull.

Ships: Inside and Outside

The interior arrangements of most medieval ships are something of a mystery. All but the smallest vessels had at least one deck, which covered the cargo hold. Bigger vessels needed two or more decks within the hull, and Henry V's 330-ton royal ship *Nicholas* of 1415 had at least two.

Ships had some cabins, but these were 'officer territory' in modern naval parlance. Cabins were only provided for important people – military commanders, the master, merchants and so on. The great ship *Trinity Royal* possessed three or more cabins and the *Holy Ghost* had at least two, with windows of some kind. In 1416, the cabin of one fleet leader – Lord Morley – even seems to have had an en-suite chapel, but few can have been this lavish.

The *Nicholas* had both cabins and 'cotes'. The latter were probably flimsy living spaces of the kind one medieval English poem labelled a 'feeble cell', a bit like the small cabins for junior officers and specialists found in Henry VIII's *Mary Rose* of 1545. We have no idea where the ordinary sailors or troops bedded down in these ships. This was long before the days of hammocks, and it's likely that the best a crewman could hope for was to sleep on a straw mattress somewhere away from the cold and the wet.

As well as sleeping, a crew had to eat. Hot food was essential for men working hard in the cold conditions at sea, so a means of cooking was needed. Some of Henry V's bigger ships seem to have had brick-built cooking furnaces, doubtless substantial *Mary Rose*-style structures sited in the hold. Metal cauldrons, cooking pots and 'kettles' are often mentioned in royal ship inventories, though it is unlikely that smaller vessels had much more than small cooking hearths.

The outside of a late medieval ship was often dominated by 'castles' – the forecastle at the bow, the aftercastle at the stern and the topcastle at the head of the mainmast. Height was a critical factor in medieval sea warfare, and it's clear that castles were developed to give vessels a height advantage in battle. The aftercastle also gave the shipmaster a useful elevated vantage point, and could provide covered space for the tiller and a cabin. It's also possible that some forecastles furnished a covered area for accommodation, but not every ship had a forecastle.

The term 'ship of forecastle' or 'ship of forestage' denoted a ship that was ready to fight. In a world with relatively few specialised sailing warships, merchantmen could easily be made ready for war by fitting a forecastle. In the late Middle Ages, the military capabilities of some ships were augmented with light wooden structures built on top of the existing castles, called a *somercastell* or *somerhuche*. The great ships *Holy Ghost* (740 tons) and *Trinity Royal* (500 tons) were fitted with these at Southampton in 1416 as part of their preparation for battle against the large Genoese carracks. We don't know how common summercastles were, but some other ships did have them, including Henry's 210-ton royal ship *Katherine*.[67]

Rig[68]

The typical north European ship of the early 1400s was one-masted and carried a square sail, an ancient technological tradition. In reality, 'square sail' simply meant a sail with four sides, not necessarily one that was actually square.

These ships sailed best with the wind blowing from the side or 'beam', though trials with a replica of the Bremen Cog (*c.* 1380) have shown that even an unwieldy looking square rigger could sail into the wind, to within 70° of the wind direction. Called sailing to windward, or sailing on a tack, this capability was important because it enabled ships to make some progress against a headwind by tacking – that is, turning across the wind direction in order to change tack. Despite this, the Cog experiments suggested that it was actually safer for these vessels to 'wear', or turn right round to get on to the other tack. This might have been less dangerous, but it would have sent a ship back on its track and cost time.

Medieval rigging can look complex, but in essence it had just two major tasks. The 'standing rigging' supported the mast and the 'running rigging'

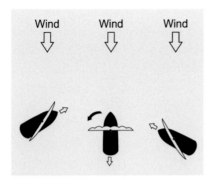

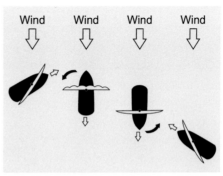

35 Tacking. 36 Wearing.

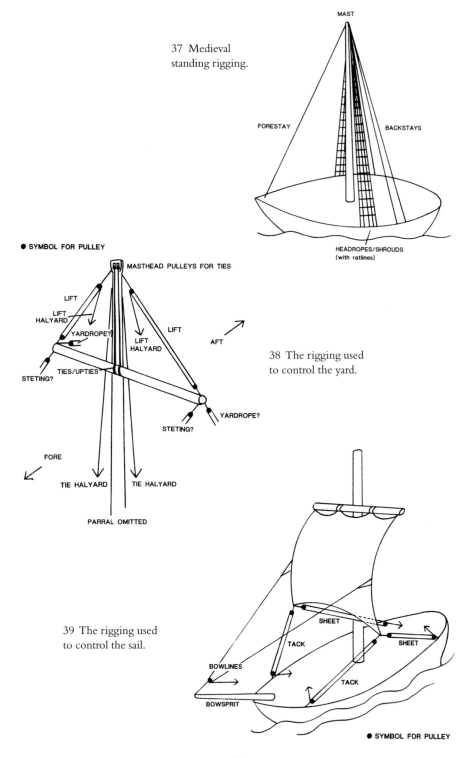

37 Medieval standing rigging.

● SYMBOL FOR PULLEY

MASTHEAD PULLEYS FOR TIES

38 The rigging used to control the yard.

39 The rigging used to control the sail.

controlled the yard and sail (see plates 37–9). Given the tendency of hemp ropes to rot, medieval sailors built redundancy into the system by rigging ropes in large numbers. Even the *Grand Gabriel*, at 180 tons not a particularly large ship, had nineteen ropes to help keep the mast in place.

Masts could be very tall. Bigger ships needed 'made masts' composed of several timbers fitted together, as beyond a certain height it was impossible to find individual trees that were tall enough (see plate 40). Sail yards or yards were usually made of one piece of timber, though at least one of Henry's great ships acquired a two-piece yard.

The yard and sail were very heavy, and raising or lowering them required a lot of muscle power, assisted by a horizontal winding drum called a windlass. In the early 1420s, the great ships *Holy Ghost* and *Jesus* were 'retrofitted' with heavy iron devices called 'flails'. The idea came from Mediterranean carracks, and the flail was used to help raise and lower yards more quickly. As well as making the job easier, it may have been a case of technology being used to make up for a shortage of sailors.

Sails were divided into two or more sections: the largest part was the body or 'course', but below this were one or more strips of canvas of the same width called 'bonnets'. The bonnets were laced on to the bottom of the course, and served as a quick way to increase or reduce sail area. A strong wind could capsize a ship

40 Part of one of a number of octagonal wooden pillars in the early fifteenth-century Wool House at Southampton. They could be sections of the core or 'spindle' of a large made mast.

carrying too much sail, and in that circumstance, a sail needed to be taken in rapidly. However, if all of the sail had to be completely furled, there was little option for the sailors but to climb up the headropes on the sides of mast, sit precariously astride the yard and shuffle out along it to pull the sail up.

The sail had to be closely controlled in order for the ship to go in the desired direction. Bowline, tacks and sheets were especially important, because they secured the bottom corners and edges of the sail. If a ship was trying to tack, the bowline on the weather edge of the sail had to be pulled tight, or the sail would collapse and the ship would wallow or get blown backwards. Manoeuvring was of course aided by a ship's stern rudder, but the steersman's efforts had to be linked to what was being done with the sail.

The limitations of one-masted square rig included its restricted ability to sail to windward, but more importantly, a one-master staked its fate on a single sail. If that sail was lost, the ship could be critically endangered. A two-masted rig was developed in the fourteenth century, in the Mediterranean, to improve the sailing qualities of great carracks, with a mizzenmast sited behind

41 A carrack-shaped one-master under sail, after an English manuscript of *c.* 1426, showing the stern rudder and a cargo port in the side (after British Library MS Cotton Tib AVII, f 81).

42 An early two-masted *cocha* under sail, after the Pizzigani chart of 1367.

the mainmast. It was smaller and carried a triangular lateen sail, which had much better windward sailing qualities than the square sail (see plate 42).

Henry V's fleet may well have led the adoption of the two-masted rig in England: between 1416 and 1420, the Crown not only started to use, but also to build two-masted ships like the balingers *George* II and *Anne* and the great ship *Jesus*. The lateen mizzen made tacking a safer manoeuvre, enhancing a ship's overall performance. The two-masted rig was an improvement, but it was soon superseded by the three-masted square rig, which added a square foresail in the bow. This made ships much more manoeuvrable, and endured until the end of the age of sail. Henry's great ship *Grace Dieu* may have been an early three-master, but there is no unambiguous evidence of the new rig in England until the mid-1430s.

How fast were medieval ships? Trials with reconstructed cogs and Viking longships have provided some answers. A replica of a German cog was able to achieve 8 knots with a Force 7 near-gale blowing on the beam, and an average of 3.4 knots in a Force 3 wind. Replicas of Viking longships have shown that they could achieve a maximum of 3.4 knots under oars and

13–15 knots under sail. For the moment, the longship data is about as close as we can get to the performance of the oared balingers and barges used in Henry V's time. It confirms what medieval people knew, both intuitively and by experience: that long, narrow and light vessels tended to be faster than heavy vessels with deep hulls. In one medieval Scandinavian legend, the royal princes Olaf and Harald raced back from Denmark to Norway on hearing of the death of their father, in order to claim the crown: the first one there would become king. They sailed in separate ships, Harald in the *Swift Dragon* and Olaf in the *Lazy Oxen*. A fourteenth-century Danish wall painting represents Harald's vessel as a longship and Olaf's as a cog, but shows the lumbering cog sailing ahead of the longship, because Olaf had divine support. He won the race, became king and was later made a saint. In other words, if a cog outpaced a longship, it was a miracle.

Speed was an asset in battle and certain other circumstances, but one wonders how significant it was for trading ships on routine voyages. Sailing ships were often at the mercy of the wind, going nowhere in light airs and perhaps hurtling in the wrong direction in strong contrary winds. At the end of December 1414, for instance, a group of royal ships *en route* from London to Bordeaux was hit by a storm off the Isle of Wight and driven back 50 miles to shelter in the Camber, the great bay near Winchelsea.

Even if the winds were not so bad, interminable tacking and wearing also ate up time and added distance. In 1412–13, the small ship *Trinity* of Bursledon (on the River Hamble) made three trips from England to Bordeaux and back, a turnaround that was a good deal faster than many of the bigger English vessels on the route. This sounds impressive, but even on its fastest passage the *Trinity* only made good around 23 sea miles per day, an average speed of just under 1 knot. The question of a 'top speed' for vessels of this time is in any case a little redundant, because merchant convoys and war fleets had to sail at the speed of the slowest ship, if they were to stay together. Most medieval sailing vessels were not 'ocean greyhounds' – they were probably closer to sea slugs.

Conservatism and Innovation

The two-masted Mediterranean rig was successfully mastered by the English. There was, however, another Mediterranean lesson in shipbuilding that they failed to learn.

43 Skeleton or 'carvel' construction.

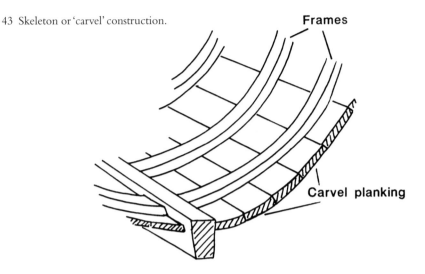

The hulls of Mediterranean ships like the carrack were built in a way that was quite different from the clinker construction of northern Europe. Mediterranean shipbuilders used skeleton or carvel construction, where a skeleton of frames was erected first, and the planks were then nailed to this. The planks were laid flush, butted against each other, not overlapping like clinker ones. The technique had been around for centuries, but was not adopted in northern Europe until the mid-fifteenth century. It's clear that the English shipwrights of Henry V's time did not have a clue as to how to repair the hulls of the captured carracks. Their craft was wedded to one kind of technology, and skeleton construction was alien to them. The government threw a lot of money at the carrack problem, and Mediterranean shipwrights were employed to undertake repairs, but it was not enough. Of seven carracks available at the end of 1417, only two remained seaworthy in 1422, and two of the other five had sunk because of their poor condition.

The conservatism of English shipwrights is in stark contrast to what appears to have been the attitude of the sailors when it came to installing a two-masted rig. English sailors were schooled in using the single square sail, but it did not define their craft, as it did with the shipwrights. This, I think, explains why they seem to have adopted helpful technology like the mizzenmast and the flail. Innovations like these didn't threaten an entrenched craft hierarchy and they might also have made sailors' hard lives a bit easier and safer.[69]

Anchors and Anchoring

Henry's bigger ships often had lots of anchors. The *Holy Ghost* (740 tons) had thirteen when first built, the carrack *George* (600 tons) carried six, as did the 180-ton sailing ship *Thomas*, but a small vessel like the 24-ton balinger *Paul* had only two. Like rigging, seafarers evidently followed a 'belt-and-braces' policy with anchors, so that if one failed, there was at least an alternative.

Anchors and cables varied considerably in weight and size. When the *Jesus* was constructed at Smallhythe in 1416–17, five huge iron anchors were made for the ship (in addition to three ready-made ones), ranging in weight from 1,624lb to 2,511lb (738–1,141kg), with eight great cables, totalling 11,564lb (5.25 tonnes). Six of the cables were each 80 fathoms or 480ft (146m) in length. The weight of the cables helped to hold the ship, and it was normal practice in later times to ensure that a cable was paid out over a distance at least four or five times the depth of the water.[70]

The shape of a typical medieval ship's anchor was very close to what became known as the 'Admiralty Pattern' anchor of later centuries (see plate 10c). The wooden stock was designed to flip the iron arms of the anchor over on the seabed, so that one of the triangular flukes would dig in. A buoy rope with a wooden buoy was attached to the anchor, so that the floating buoy would mark its position and warn others not to anchor there.[71]

The combination of an anchor with an anchor cable could be very heavy, and they were raised or lowered by a windlass (or capstan, a vertical winding drum) powered by the strong arms and backs of the crew. Raised pairs of anchors were normally secured horizontally on either side of the forecastle by an arrangement of ropes, chains and hooks.

The 1,400-ton *Grace Dieu* carried one of the biggest iron objects produced in medieval England, a Southampton-made anchor with a shank 17ft 2in (5.23m) long and arms that were 11ft 5in (3.48m) wide. This valuable anchor and another one were measured in the early 1450s so that they could be loaned to a private ship. The other anchor was not much smaller and had its own name, *Marie Tynktawe*. It had been around since at least 1411, going to sea successively in the *Trinity Royal* and the *Holy Ghost*. A lot of hope was invested in anchors, so giving one a religious dedication was not that odd.

Ships' Boats

Every ship of any size had its own boat, whether it was a small 'cockboat' or one of the 'great boats' or followers used by the bigger vessels (see plate 11c). The cockboats might have been carried on deck, but great boats would be towed behind, because of their size. In 1413, the *Cog John* had a great boat with twenty-six oars, a mast and a sail, as well as an eight-oared cockboat.

Three of the great ships' boats, those of the *Jesus*, *Holy Ghost* and *Trinity Royal*, were either rebuilt or reclassified as balingers (see Appendix 2).[72] These humble oared craft were absolutely essential for landing operations like the Normandy invasions of 1415 and 1417, because the landing sites lacked quays and beaching a transport ship was risky (see Chapter 6).

Types of Ships

Medieval vessels belonged to two general kinds, known to historians and archaeologists as the 'round ship', a relatively deep-hulled sailing craft, and the 'longship', a long, narrow and low-hulled vessel that could move under both sail and oars. This division was more or less clear in Henry V's royal fleet, which fielded five main types. Three of these were 'round ships': great ships, ships and carracks. The other two types were oared vessels, balingers and barges. The word 'ship' can sometimes be problematic in this context. Rendered as *navis* in Latin or *nef* in medieval Norman French, it was used both as a generic term for something larger than a boat and, apparently, as the name of a particular type.[73] The type names given to vessels in the accounts of the king's ships did not change very much once they were in royal ownership.

Carracks and Great Ships

The easiest of the royal vessels to characterise are the Genoese carracks. Henry's forces captured eight of them in the battles of 1416 and 1417, and at least four of these were used operationally by the English. The carrack was a type first developed in Italy in the late thirteenth and early fourteenth century. It combined Mediterranean skeleton construction with the capacious hull form, stern rudder and square sail of the north European cog. Called a *cocha* in Italy and other places, the vessel was a bulk carrier, and its great size also made it useful as a warship.[74]

In the last few decades of the thirteenth century, Venetian and Genoese galleys pioneered the long and arduous trade route from the Mediterranean to Flanders and England. The galley cargoes were typically low-volume luxury goods, but *coche* were later also used in the trade as bulk carriers for cargoes like alum, a dye fixative in demand in the north European cloth industries. After 1340, the Genoese replaced all of their galleys on the northern route with *coche*. The English and other northerners began to call these big ships 'carracks'; the origin of the term is uncertain, but it stuck. The carrack became a byword for a very large ship, familiar enough to the late fourteenth-century English for Geoffrey Chaucer's Summoner in the *Canterbury Tales* to say that Satan's tail was wider than a carrack's sail.[75]

The overall shape of a carrack is well known from fourteenth- and fifteenth-century images and other sources. Its hull was wide and deep, with a high, curved stem that made the forecastle higher than the aftercastle. The hull also had a great deal of 'tumblehome', that is, the sides curved inwards in their upper parts. Italian figures from the fifteenth century suggest that in carracks the ratio between keel length and hull width (beam) was somewhere between 1:2.25 and 1:3, creating a tubby hull ideally suited for bulk goods. To put this in some sort of context, a long, narrow oared warship like the contemporary English balinger might have a keel/beam ratio of perhaps 1:4 or more.[76] The Mataro Model (see plate 12c)[77] is probably the best representation of a medieval carrack that we will ever see, and gives a good general impression of what Henry's captured Genoese carracks looked like. Carracks normally had two or three decks, besides those in the superstructures, to allow them to carry large amounts of cargo. The great height of these vessels made carracks formidable in war.

The 1416–17 carracks were not the first ships of this kind owned by the English Crown. A two-masted Genoese carrack was seized by the government in 1410, after pirates had captured it in Milford Haven the previous year. Originally called the *Sancta Maria & Sancta Brigida*, the ship was known simply as *Le Carake* in English service.

This was the period when Prince Henry dominated the royal council: he was probably behind the growth of the royal fleet around this time, and could no doubt see the warlike potential of a big ship like *Le Carake*. Unfortunately, this carrack was wrecked off the Isle of Wight on a return voyage from Bordeaux in late 1411 or early 1412. Some of its gear and cargo was washed ashore, and the salvaged mainmast seems to have been recycled for use in Henry's great ship *Holy Ghost*.[78]

There is a real possibility, I feel, that the idea for Henry V's four 'great ships' came from this ill-fated carrack. *Le Carake* would have made most English ships look very small, and even though the 1411–12 voyage ended badly, it did show that the English were able to operate a carrack on a long voyage. The very size of *Le Carake* also made it a potent symbol of royal power, no mean thing in an era that took symbolism very seriously. The great ships functioned exactly as war carracks did, it is clear that they were, in effect, clinker-built versions of carracks.

Ships

The shapes of the other royal sailing ships are far less easy to interpret than those of the carracks. Some of them may have looked like small-scale carracks: certainly the carrack hull form featured in north European imagery by the early fifteenth century (see plates 41, 44 and 16c), and medieval images of ships often reflected the reality in some way. What we do know from the written, archaeological and visual sources is that a variety of types existed in late medieval England and northern Europe.

The most famous type was the cog, with its broad, deep, flat-bottomed hull and distinctive angular stem and sternposts. Cogs were ubiquitous in the Baltic and North Sea in the thirteenth and fourteenth centuries, and were still very much around in Henry V's day. Large numbers of the vessels hired from Holland and Zeeland to transport his invasion armies in 1415 and 1417 were described as 'cogships'.

We don't know, though, if any of Henry's own ships were cogs. Two of them were called *Cog John* and the *Rodcogge*, and the obvious assumption is that they *were* cogs. The problem is, the word 'cog' sometimes featured in the names of English oared vessels, that were utterly unlike the trading ship, so 'cog' in a ship's name is not necessarily a clue to its type.

Henry also briefly owned a one-masted ship called the *Marie Hulke*. 'Hulk' or 'hulc' could denote a specific type or method of construction. Sometimes, though, it was used to describe vessels that belonged to the German Hanseatic League. Perhaps the *Marie Hulke* was of Baltic origin, and the name reflected this. One thing we can be sure of is that all the ships in the royal fleet that came from northern Europe or northern Iberia were

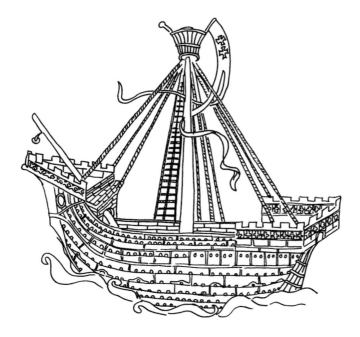

44 Cog? Hulk? 'Ship'? This vessel on the seal of Gdansk, or Danzig, of *c.* 1400 has features in common with a cog, a hulk and a carrack. (after Ewe, 1972, no. 53)

clinker-built. The technique was ubiquitous in these regions until carvel construction began to supplant it in the mid-1400s.[79]

The configurations of the smaller types of English vessels are even more elusive than those of the 'ships' in the royal fleet. Conscripted small craft like crayers and picards were one-masters and some can be identified as merchantmen from their functions, but their shapes remain unknown.[80]

Oared Fighting Ships

Henry's oared war fleet consisted of balingers and barges, although the former greatly outnumbered the latter. In some senses, we know exactly what these vessels were. They could move under sail as well as oars, they were of relatively low tonnage, and they were fast and manoeuvrable when compared with vessels driven only by sail. As oared ships, they needed to be long, narrow, low-built and light, to accommodate a rowing crew, to enable the oars to reach the water, and to make the most of the power developed by the rowers.

From the mid-1300s onwards, barges and balingers supplanted the galley as the primary English oared fighting vessel, at least in name. The word 'balinger' is said to have come from the Old French *baleinier*, meaning a fast, oared whaling boat, though other possible etymologies have been suggested. There are indications that barges tended to be bigger than balingers, but Henry's great 120-ton balingers *Anne*, *George* and *Nicholas* were almost as big as any medieval barge on record. Just to confuse the issue, medieval people sometimes used the two different type names for the same ship. Most of Henry's oared fighting vessels were called balingers in the sources, however, and it's pointless to become obsessed with the distinction. Some 'civilian' balingers were used for trade (as were some of Henry's), but the balinger's agility and its ability to move independently of the wind made it especially useful in war and piracy.

Balingers could be tiny. The *Katherine Breton*, for instance, had a crew of eleven and just eight oars, though we don't know its tonnage. We do, however, know the tonnages for thirteen of the eighteen or so oared warships owned by Henry, and these fall into three rough groups by size:

Tonnage	No. of vessels	No. of oars	Crew size
20–40	7	20–34	24–43
50–80	2	38–48	51–91
100–20	4	24–71	50–143

There wasn't necessarily a direct relationship between tonnage and the numbers of oars: the 56-ton *Craccher* had forty-eight oars, the 80-ton *Falcon* had only thirty-eight and the 120-ton *Nicholas* seems to have possessed a mere twenty-four. Crew sizes could vary considerably, suggesting that on some voyages, vessels did not ship their full set of oars, or they were only used under sail. Mostly, though, there were enough men for all the oars. In 1413, the 24-ton *Paul* went to sea with one man for each of the twenty-four oars. At the other end of the scale, the 120-ton balinger *George* II had around seventy oars and on at least one occasion carried a crew of 143, making it possible to man each oar with two men. The *George* is described rather enigmatically as having been built 'in the manner of a galley', which in early fifteenth-century English terms most likely meant a Mediterranean-style galley. It's possible that putting two men to each oar was thought of as Mediterranean practice.[81]

45 Conjectural sketch
of a balinger.

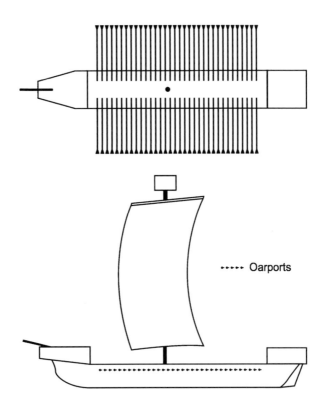

Balinger - conjectural sketch

The oars were probably shipped through ports cut in the top row of planking (see plate 45). As the balinger *Anne* had a keel length of 68ft (20.7m) and carried sixty-eight oars (thirty-four on a side), it is a reasonable presumption that the oar ports were 2ft (0.6m) apart. The oars themselves were quite big: those supplied for this balinger were 24ft long (7.3m). The image (plate 45) gives a rough sketch of what a balinger may have looked like, with a single mast and conjectured low superstructures.[82]

5

MACHINES OF WAR

The War Machine: Platforms and Weaponry

Weapons are listed in the inventories of thirty-one of the forty-six operational royal ships. Any soldiers who were embarked brought their own arms with them, so the inventoried weapons must have been intended for use by the crew (see Appendix 4). Conversely, the absence of weapons from a ship's inventory – including that of the great ship *Jesus* – does not mean that it was never used in combat operations. In such situations, a vessel's main 'firepower' normally came from the men-at-arms and archers it carried.

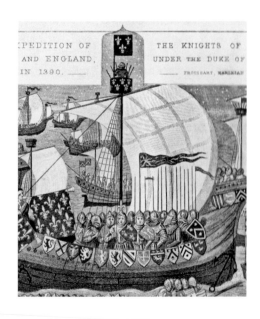

46 A soldier and gads in a ship's topcastle (after Nicolas 1847, p.386).

The fighting platforms within a late medieval ship were the forecastle and aftercastle (together with any summercastles erected on top of them), the weather deck between the castles and the topcastle at the head of the mast (see also plate 16c).[83]

Topcastles or 'tops' were accessed via the shrouds on either side of the mast, and the tops on larger ships had room for several men. Weapons such as arrows or spears could be projected from tops, but in the late medieval period there was also a specialised weapon designed specifically for the top – the gad. Deriving from a Germanic word that probably meant 'a spike', the word survives in the modern English 'gadfly'. Gads were long, sharpened iron spears. They are commonly found in images of medieval ships, sticking out of topcastles like so many toothpicks (see plate 46), and they were used on at least ten of Henry's ships. Information on gads purchased for the royal ships in the early 1420s suggests that their average weight ranged from about 8lb to 18lb (3.6–8.2kg), although there may well have been heavier examples. They were aimed and thrown, and fell with enough force to penetrate plate armour. The 'darts' found in some ship inventories may have been a smaller version of the gad, perhaps with flights of some kind to stabilise them.[84]

Armaments were lifted up to the tops by means of light ropes called 'cranelines', worked by small cranes or winches attached to the topcastle itself. It was common for Henry's ships to have two cranelines, which must have sped up the job of rearming the top. Lumps of rock were also used as makeshift weapons in tops, winched up in cloth bags or nets.[85]

If one weapon in particular is associated with Henry V's reign, it is the longbow. This is because of the famous part played in the battle of Agincourt by English archers. Due to fourteenth-century English legislation, which made regular archery practice compulsory for men, the country had a lot of skilled archers, and a huge store of bows, arrows and other archery equipment. Our understanding of medieval archery has been greatly enhanced by the discovery of a large number of longbows, arrows and archers' gear in the wreck of the *Mary Rose* (sunk 1545).

English bows were made of yew, and those from the *Mary Rose* measured nearly 6.5ft (1.97m) in length. Arrows were packed in sheaves of at least 24 units, held together by leather spacers. Using the 24-arrow sheaf as a measure, ships like the *Grand Marie* carried 600 or more arrows, the carrack *George* had 2,664, and even the small (20-ton) balinger *Swan* had 288.

Experiments with replica *Mary Rose* bows have shown that heavier types of arrows could fly for at least 220m, though the range would probably need

47 Shipboard archers and cannon, after a late fifteenth-century manuscript (British Library, Cotton MS Julius EIV, f 18v). The foremost archer seems to be wearing a *jakke* (a padded jacket).

to be between 18 and 91m for them to seriously wound or kill an opponent. We know very little about how bows were actually used in ships in the early fifteenth century, but these figures suggest that shipborne archery was a fairly close-range affair. The sheer size of a longbow, and the need for space to fire at a high angle means that it is likely that archers were normally deployed on the open deck in the waist or on the upper castle decks.[86]

Crossbows were rare as part of the standard equipment of the Henry's ships, though forty-seven 'small coffers for quarrels for carracks' had found their way into the royal storehouse by 1420, and were probably once used by the Genoese crossbowmen in the battles of 1416 and 1417. Crossbows were powerful weapons and could be fired from enclosed spaces under the castle decks, but their rate of fire must have been considerably slower than that of bows, because of the time needed to wind up the crossbow string before firing.[87]

The only other 'small arms' carried in any numbers by royal ships were lances or spears, and poleaxes. The lances and spears could have been thrown, but the likelihood is that they were intended for close combat, either for repelling boarders or for carving a way on to another ship. Poleaxes were small axes or hatchets, used in naval warfare to cut an enemy ship's rigging or to brain its crewmen. Hand weapons were issued mainly to Henry's great ships and ships, and seldom featured in the inventories of the carracks or oared vessels, though it is quite likely that many sailors would have had their own swords or daggers.

Guns or cannon were not common in Henry's ships. They had first been used at sea in the 1330s, but would not be carried in large numbers by ships until the second half of the fifteenth century. Only fifteen of Henry V's ships had them, sharing a total of forty-two guns. The terms 'gun' and 'cannon' were used interchangeably, giving little clue as to specific type, though most of these weapons were breech-loaders, with powder carried in a separate breech chamber. A gun would often have more than one breech chamber, to ensure that a charge was ready to hand for reloading. The guns were usually made of iron, where stated, though there are references to guns made of brass or bronze. The only ammunition mentioned consisted of gunstones, probably made of Kentish ragstone like the gunstones found in the *Mary Rose* (Henry V ordered large numbers of stone cannonballs from the Maidstone and Hythe areas).

Most of the guns were on sailing vessels – great ships, carracks and ships. The only gun-armed oared vessel was the balinger *Roose*, which already had two breech-loaders when acquired in 1420. The 'heaviest' gun armament in

48 Soldiers and guns on a ship carved on Greenway Chapel, Tiverton, Devon, 1517. Although this image post-dates Henry V's time by a century and shows a three-masted ship, the arrangement of men-at-arms and guns is little different from the fifteenth century: the men wear armour, the soldier in the centre carries a poleaxe, and the guns fire over the gunwale.

49 Breech-loading swivel guns, on replica mounts, found in the sea near Venice and dated to the fifteenth century. (Courtesy of the Museo Storico Navale di Venezia, © Ian Friel 2011)

Henry's fleet was aboard the great ship *Holy Ghost*, which had seven guns and a dozen chambers, though it lost one of its guns in the 1417 battle.

There is no indication as to whether Henry's naval guns were mounted on wheeled wooden carriages or on swivels. The references to stone shot may suggest that these were the larger carriage-mounted types, but one cannot be certain.

The carrack *George* was supplied with three breech-loaders for the Earl of Huntingdon's expedition in 1417, along with seventy-two gunstones and 65lb (29.5kg) of gunpowder (there were also seventy-two tampions – wooden plugs – for the six breech chambers). The gunpowder allowance per shot averaged at just under 14.5oz (0.4kg), a charge for a fairly small weapon in sixteenth-century terms, so it seems that the *George*'s guns did not pack much of a punch.

There were perhaps just two medieval weapons that were specifically 'naval'. One was the gad, the other was the iron grapnel, used to hook and hold an enemy ship so that it could be boarded (see plate 50). Fourteen of Henry's vessels carried these, though all bar two were sailing ships or carracks. Of the oared vessels, only the balingers *Anne* and *Craccher* had them. Most ships only had one grapnel, but the *Holy Ghost* had two, each attached to iron chains 12 fathoms (72ft or 22m) in length. It lost one of these grapnels and its chain when they fell into the sea during the 1416 battle of Harfleur.

A few royal ships carried crew armour or other protective clothing. In 1413, the *Thomas* had eighteen *bascinets* (helmets) with visors, ten breastplates

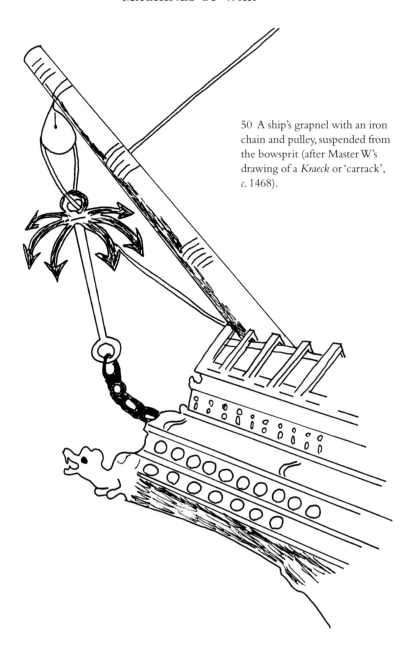

50 A ship's grapnel with an iron chain and pulley, suspended from the bowsprit (after Master W's drawing of a *Kraeck* or 'carrack', *c.* 1468).

and nine sets of leg-armour, all stored in a barrel. The ship *Little Trinity* and the balinger *Paul* had a few *jakkes* (padded jackets), but most vessels had no armour for the crew at all. Perhaps the sailors found it too heavy and constricting for fighting in the close confines of a vessel.[88]

The Royal Ships in Battle

Apart from the two big battles of Harfleur (1416) and the Chef de Caux (1417), we don't know how often Henry V's royal ships actually fought. The administrative records of the fleet are not much help here. Aside from the capture of some individual vessels, the only two actions they refer to are the battles of 1416 and 1417. The accounts do list the disposal of weapons and ammunition over three periods, 1413–16, 1416–20 and 1420–22, but they seldom explain why or how these items ceased to be the king's property.

It is possible, however, that some of these accounting exercises actually conceal the use of weapons in otherwise-unrecorded actions at sea. For instance, between 1413 and 1416 there were numerous trading voyages in which the royal ships probably also functioned as convoy escorts, as well as two war operations and a fishery protection cruise. During this period, six ships (*Cog John, Grand Marie, Katherine, Little Trinity, Rodcogge* and *Thomas*) and two balingers (*Peter* and *Paul*) between them expended 55 sheaves of arrows (at least 1,320 arrows), 102 darts, 39 hand weapons and 1 grapnel. The *Thomas* also used up 20 gunstones, as did the *Little Trinity* (though the evidence for guns on the latter ship is not otherwise clear). Likewise, between 1416 and 1420 the great ships *Holy Ghost* and *Trinity Royal* somehow disposed of over 800 arrows, 45 gads and 60 darts, many of these perhaps used in the 1416 and 1417 battles. Although it would be naïve to think that all of these items disappeared in combat with enemy ships, it would be equally simplistic to think that they all merely fell overboard, rotted away or were sold off by enterprising sailors.[89]

The Tactics of Sea Warfare

The details of the two major sea battles of Henry V's reign are not very clear, but chronicles and other sources do record some of the tactics used by medieval seafarers and these may help us to understand these battles a little better. The 1416 and 1417 battles took place just off the coast, a common feature in actions from Damme (1213) and Sluys (1340) to Zonchio (1499). The reason for this is that it was easier to locate an enemy force when it was in sight of land. Attacks were often 'intelligence-based', in that one side knew roughly where the other was to be found and relied on following coastal features in order to locate the enemy. Geographical reference points were of course not available out of sight of land, and encounters on the high seas were rare, and accidental (this made the English seakeeping operations of 1415 to 1421 something of a shot in the dark when it came to finding enemy fleets).

Manoeuvring to attack was of course a normal part of combat, using wind and currents – or the lack of them – to gain an advantage over an adversary. An English fleet made sure that it got to windward of a French one off Dover in 1217, gaining 'the weather gage' (as it was called in later centuries) because it allowed them to choose when and where to attack. Conversely, in a 1406 battle out in the English Channel, a force of Spanish oared galleys and balingers used the opportunity of calm weather to attack a group of English ships, because the Spanish could move easily under oars, without the wind.

Ramming was commonplace in the 1416–17 battles (see Chapter 7), though to do this an attacker needed the windward position in order to gain greater impetus. It was, quite literally, a shock tactic. It brought both ships to a sudden halt, probably knocked the enemy crew off their feet and quite possibly destroyed the forecastle or rigging of the target ship. In the 1406 battle, a Spanish balinger smashed into an English balinger and 'took out' its bowsprit and forestay, causing the mast to collapse. In 1440, the 320-ton *Christopher* of Dartmouth ploughed into the 120-ton *George* of Wells under

51 (Left) Tactics: getting the weather gage, or moving to windward. Drawing any tactical diagram for this period involves a great deal of conjecture, but these images offer possible examples of what may have been done.

52 (Right) Tactics: ramming. The attacking ship turns at 'a' and hits the bow of its target at 'b'.

Wind

53 (Left) Tactics:
bombardment with
arrows, crossbow bolts
and cannon shot.

Wind

54 (Right) Tactics:
boarding. The
ships are chained
bow-to-bow ('a').

a sail that was filled 'by a large wind' (spelling modernised), and the 'foreship' of the smaller vessel collapsed into the water. Immobilising a ship made it vulnerable to capture: this could be achieved by ramming, but it was also something that attackers tried to do when they boarded a ship, by cutting the rigging ropes.

Boarding was usually preceded by a bombardment of arrows and other projectiles, to kill or maim sailors on the open decks and clear the way for the boarders. Most medieval naval battles ended with a series of boarding actions, in which ships were grappled together and their crews fought more or less as they would in a land battle. The only differences were that the shipboard battlefield was tiny, filled with a deadly hail falling from the topcastles above and there was an ever-present danger of drowning. Ships and their contents were items of value as prizes, and this is why in many battles the key objective was to capture, rather than sink, enemy vessels. Sometimes, though, the tactical imperative was simply to destroy enemy shipping, and fire was needed for this, as at La Rochelle in 1372 and in the aftermath of the battle of Harfleur.[90]

There's always a danger of reading history backwards by trying to interpret one century by using sources from the next, but there is reason to think that early to mid-sixteenth-century writings on naval tactics can tell us something about those of the fifteenth century. Although broadside-firing warships with heavy guns like the *Mary Rose* were developed in the early 1500s, it wasn't until the second half of the sixteenth century that sailors really began to work out how to use them most effectively.[91] Before this, big guns were seen as an adjunct to existing (medieval) tactics and not as weapons that transformed the nature of war at sea.

In the first half of the sixteenth century, the Spanish seaman Alonso de Chaves set down a number of principles for sea fighting, often using analogies derived from land warfare. The 'strongest and largest ships' in a fleet would be tasked to 'attack, grapple, board and break-up the enemy', like 'men-at-arms … to make and meet charges'. The 'weaker ships' would be separate from these, 'with their artillery and munitions to harass, pursue, and give chase to the enemy if he flies, and to come to the rescue whenever there is most need'. Fleets were to sail in line abreast (a formation used by the English in the 1406 battle), with the biggest ships in the centre, as they would have enemies on both sides when the action was joined. The lighter vessels were to position themselves to windward, so that they could see where help was needed most. Trumpets and flag signals would signal the attack. Heavy guns would serve to intimidate the enemy from longer range, but as soon as ships were grappled together, projectiles, darts (*dardos*), stones, hand guns and other weapons would be let loose, and attempts would be made to cut the sails and rigging of the enemy.[92]

English fighting instructions of around 1530 had a lot of similarities with those of Chaves, though there were differences in detail. The importance of the 'weather gage' was emphasised from the start: 'If they meet with the enemy, the admiral must apply to get the wind of the enemy by all means he can, for that is the advantage.' Ships were to seek out vessels of roughly equal size for boarding: 'Let every ship match equally as near as they can, and leave some pinnaces (lighter vessels) at liberty to help the overmatched.' Boarding was to be delayed until the heavy guns had been fired, along with lighter guns and crossbow shot (and also, presumably, arrows). The aim of the bombardment was to clear the enemy decks of defenders, or at least, of men capable of fighting. If an enemy ship had been boarded, but one of their vessels came to its aid, the ship was to be scuttled, first ensuring that the English had got back to their own ship, taking 'the captain and certain of the best with him' – the human capital of ransom. The rest of the enemy crew was to be 'committed to the sea, for else they will turn upon you to your confusion'.[93]

These medieval battle accounts and sixteenth-century sources help to illuminate some of the evidence for the great clashes of Henry's day. This makes it possible to get a better sense of what was 'going on' in sea battles and other operations even if the exact order of events is not always clear.

The division between the roles of sailing ships and lighter oared vessels in combat described by the sixteenth-century tacticians is perceptible in the planned composition of a 1418 seakeeping fleet. In 1418, Sir John Arundel made an indenture to serve at sea as the lieutenant of Thomas Beaufort, Duke of Exeter, the Admiral of England. The seakeeping voyage was due to start from Southampton on 1 April that year, and last for six months. Arundel would supply a retinue of three knights, 364 men-at-arms and 776 archers.[94] The original plan was that fleet would consist of five sailing ships, including three royal carracks, with ten oared balingers and barges. The size and composition of the force proved to be slightly different in actuality, but the indenture reveals some of the commanders' thinking about tactics:

Ship(s)	Tons	Master	Crew size	Men-at -arms	Archers
Peter, royal carrack	600	John Gerard	approx. 100	80	160
Christopher, royal carrack	600	William Tenderley	approx. 100	60	120
George, royal carrack	600	William Richeman	approx. 100	60	120
Ship of forestage★ (1)	nk	nk	nk	36	72
Ship of forestage★ (2)	nk	nk	nk	36	72
Barge (1)	nk	nk	nk	20	40
Barge (2)	nk	nk	nk	20	40
Barge (3)	nk	nk	nk	20	40
Barge (4)	nk	nk	nk	20	40
Balinger (1)	nk	nk	nk	2	12
Balinger (2)	nk	nk	nk	2	12
Balinger (3)	nk	nk	nk	2	12
Balinger (4)	nk	nk	nk	2	12
Balinger (5)	nk	nk	nk	2	12
Balinger (6)	nk	nk	nk	2	12

★ rendered as *mese de forscage* in the catalogue entry, but should be read as *niefs de forstage*, i.e. 'ships with a forecastle'.

The soldiers were allocated in this way:

	Men-at-arms (%)	Archers (%)
Sailing vessels	74.7	71.4
Barges	22.0	20.6
Balingers	0.3	9.3

Nearly three-quarters of the fighting power of the military component of the force was in the sailing vessels. This sounds very much like the sixteenth-century division between the large fighting ships, which fought boarding actions, and the supporting oared wings, suggesting that this tactical arrangement was also normal in Henry V's time.

The allocation of the two kinds of soldier is also significant. The barges each had enough men-at-arms to fight an action against another smaller vessel, or to support one of the big ships in a boarding action, but the balingers did not. Archers provided their main weaponry, which indicates that they were there to give mobile supporting fire for the big ships, rather than to take on other vessels in hand-to-hand combat. In 1420, substantial numbers of bows and arrows were supplied to royal balingers in another seakeeping expedition, pointing to a similar planned tactical usage (see Appendix 4).

It was difficult for low-built vessels to overcome large ships, as an episode from 1416 shows. On Thursday 24 September 1416, a Genoese carrack was spotted sailing between Calais and Dover, under full sail and heading north. The Captain of Calais, the Earl of Warwick, and several other aristocrats, hastily crewed and armed six balingers. They set off in hot pursuit, even though the carrack had disappeared from sight by the time they left harbour. One vessel lost company with the other five, but at dawn on the Friday the remaining balingers found the carrack and attacked it. They grappled with the Genoese ship, even though its deck was a lance-length higher than any deck in the balingers. They took turns to draw off from the fight, in order to rest their crews, and fought until almost nightfall. It is said that they were on the point of winning when lack of projectiles forced them to give up and let the carrack escape. This was undoubtedly a fierce and bloody action, with dead and wounded on both sides: when the carrack finally made port, only four of its 62-man crew remained unwounded. All of the English balingers eventually got home.

The story is given in Henry V's earliest biography, the *Gesta Henrici Quinti*, possibly written by his confessor, Stephen Patrington (Bishop of Chichester from 1417). This tale of a gallant English failure gets more attention in the *Gesta* than the victory at Harfleur a few weeks earlier, probably because the author saw it as exemplifying the courage and determination of the aristocracy. It is obvious that there was bravery aplenty, but the men who led the operation embarked on it with insufficient ammunition, no scaling ladders and little or no food. However, whether one sees this as an epic sea-chase or the sorry tale of a bunch of incompetent 'Hooray Henrys' bent on violence, loot and glory, it did show how challenging it was for small ships to take a carrack.[95]

But it was not impossible. In 1418, the crews of seven English boats called picards captured a 300-ton Genoese carrack off the north Devon coast. Picards were very small. They were sailing lighters of some kind, primarily used to carry the catches from fishing boats at sea to port.[96] Needless to say, the achievement of these men was not celebrated by any chroniclers.

6

THE SEA-ROAD TO AGINCOURT AND BEYOND, 1413–15

Ever since Sir Nicholas Harris Nicolas published the two medieval volumes of his *History of the Royal Navy* in 1847, Henry V has been recognised as one of the few medieval English kings who really understood how to use sea power to get what he wanted.[97] He became king on 21 March 1413. Along with the kingdom, he inherited a moribund royal fleet of just four vessels, only two of which were functional, the barge *Marie* and the balinger *Gabriel*. A new clerk of the king's ships was appointed, William Loveney, but he did not receive or spend any money and lasted just under four months in office. The only royal ship activity in this period was the despatch of the barge *Marie de la Toure* to Portugal around May 1413, carrying an ambassador. The vessel is not mentioned again in the sources, and does not seem to be the same as the later royal ship *Little Marie* (Appendix 2).[98]

Loveney's successor as clerk of the king's ships was William Catton, who took office on 18 July. His arrival was followed by a flurry of activity: in less than a week, five vessels were acquired for the king. These were the ships *Little Marie* (80 tons), the *Little Trinity* (120 tons) and *Thomas* (180 tons), along with the 24-ton balingers *Peter* and *Paul*. The *Cog John* also officially joined the royal fleet.[99] None of these ships were built for the Crown, though it is likely that they were fairly new, as they all saw heavy service over the next few years.[100]

Acquisitions of ships continued over the next couple of years, although unfortunately we don't know where most of them originated. These were the ships *Rodcogge* (120 tons), *Grand Marie* (116/140 tons), *Philip* (130 tons),

Katherine (210 tons) and *Nicholas* (330 tons). The first of the great ships, the *Trinity Royal* (500 tons), also joined the fleet. It was the only one of these ships actually constructed for the king, rebuilt at Greenwich from the old *Trinity*, and floated out of its dock in February 1415.

Over the same period, four vessels were lost or disposed of: the *Cog John* sank off Brittany in October 1414 and the balinger *Paul* was wrecked during a seakeeping patrol between February and April 1415. The old balinger *Gabriel* came back to Sandwich after the same voyage, but then disappears from the records. The king's only other balinger, the *Peter*, was given away at about the same time.

The royal fleet of the years 1413–15 consisted mainly of sailing ships. But what was it actually meant to do? One of its shorter-term aims, I suggest, was to support Henry's efforts to make the sea safer for trade and fishing. English waters had become chaotic in Henry IV's time, with the rise in privateering and piracy. Piracy was not made a felony until 1536, but it could be seen as an offence against the king's peace if the targets of sea robbery happened to be from a country with which England had a treaty, or they were travelling under a safe conduct issued by the king. For this reason, the Statute of Truces, passed at the 1414 Parliament at Leicester, made attacks on such shipping an act of treason. As Christopher Allmand observes, Henry had been concerned

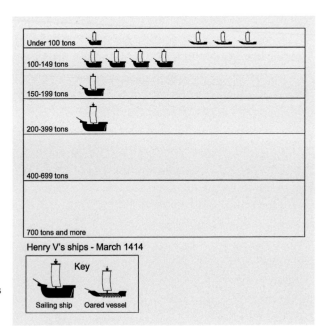

55 Operational vessels in the royal fleet in March 1414.

to establish stability at sea in the interests of trade since at least 1410. There were complaints in Parliament about the level of attacks in shipping, and to an extent the Statute was a response to those protests. It was also an expression of the king's desire for his own kind of good governance, as well as the need to prevent piratical attacks from turning Burgundy or Brittany into enemies. The Statute proposed to set up a 'conservator of truces' in each port, drawn from substantial local landowners and paid the very good salary of £40 per year – clearly, the aim was to fill the posts with men who were less easy to intimidate or corrupt. The system was well thought out, designed to increase the security of ships under royal protection, and to ensure that the perpetrators of any attacks on such vessels were punished. However, there is no evidence that the scheme was ever implemented. There are no known sets of conservators' records, and no sign that any conservators were appointed. For all that, the Statute seems to have had a deterrent effect of some kind. English merchants and sailors later claimed that the spirit of the legislation inhibited them from striking back at foreign pirates, undermining English common law rights and the tradition of reprisal.[101]

Henry was taking steps to try to protect trade even before the Statute was passed in May 1414, using his own ships and making some money at the same time by carrying commercial cargoes. The majority of voyages undertaken by

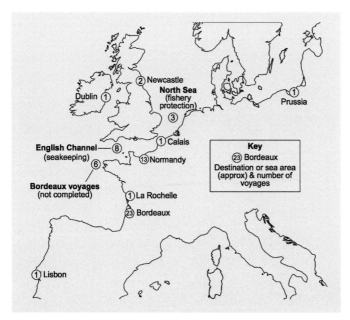

56 The voyages of the royal ships, 1413–16.

Henry's ships in the years 1413–16 were for the carriage of cargo, and most of these were to Bordeaux. The practice continued right through the king's reign, and some royal ships were heading for Gascony at the time he died. However, there is evidence that this was not just a moneymaking scheme, or a way of keeping ships busy. On 26 August 1413, an order was sent out to all the seaports in the kingdom preventing anyone from sailing to Bordeaux unless they went in the company of 'other armed ships in sufficient number and power' to deter attacks by foreign vessels. Just a week or so later, four royal ships set off for Bordeaux. I think that the intention here was to use them as convoy escorts as well as merchantmen; given the frequency with which royal vessels sailed on the route, it is very likely that the policy continued throughout Henry's reign. A convoy system was commonly used in the Gascon trade, and the royal ships would have offered additional protection.[102]

The wine trade was not the only one receiving protection. In 1413, John Bohun of Sussex was paid £20 to equip two balingers and to go to sea between 8 September and 1 November to safeguard English ships taking wool and other goods to Calais, and those making the return voyage. Bohun was also instructed to protect fishermen and other English subjects at sea.[103] A fishery protection operation was also entrusted to three royal balingers, the *Gabriel*, *Peter* and *Paul*, which sailed on a month-long mission in the North Sea at the end of September 1413. As the balingers did not go with full war crews, the aim was to deter potential aggressors rather than fight. Some of those aggressors were probably Scots: seven years later, the December 1420 Parliament complained of 'daily' Scottish attacks on English fishermen. Apart from the 1413 operation and a small seakeeping patrol in 1418, however, Henry did little to 'police' the North Sea, and it doesn't seem to have been very high on his list of priorities.[104]

Exactly when Henry V decided to go to war with France is not certain. France was passing through a period of great instability when Henry became king, with rival factions of the nobility at each other's throats and a Valois monarch who was prone to periods of madness. The situation was ripe for exploitation by outsiders. Henry tried diplomacy, demanding areas of French territory and the hand of Princess Katherine of France, but negotiation did not get him very far, and perhaps he didn't expect it to. Henry V may have been thinking of war as early as June 1413, and in 1414 he was certainly stockpiling weapons and ammunition. He also negotiated with John the Fearless, Duke of Burgundy, to secure an alliance, or at least to gain a free hand in his dealings with France. Duke John was a member of the French royal family, with a powerbase in parts of eastern France and the Low Countries. His support would later prove crucial in obtaining invasion transports from the Dutch ports.[105]

Until 1415, the activities of Henry's royal ships were defensive in nature. The acquisition of more ships was perhaps one indicator of aggressive intent, but there was a much more obvious sign of this in the king's shipbuilding activities. Work started on the great ship *Trinity Royal* in 1413 and on its larger (740-ton) counterpart the *Holy Ghost* in 1414. Although they were floating symbols of Henry's prestige and power, they had just one practical use: war.[106]

The intention to go to war was effectively made public at the Parliament of November 1414. The king had to get the agreement of Members to vote taxes to fund the massive expenses of conflict. Parliament's response was marked by some reluctance, but the king got what he wanted. Although the diplomatic process would continue into 1415, its true purpose seems to have been to demonstrate to the world – and to God – that Henry had tried every peaceful avenue before embarking on the road to war.[107]

Henry's royal fleet suffered its first loss in early October 1414. The *Cog John* sank in a storm on the coast of Brittany, but the sinking made no difference to the operations of the royal ships. As 1414 ended, the *Little Trinity* and *Philip* completed a trip from Bordeaux to London. They arrived on 27 December, but, in a remarkably short turnaround, on 30 December they were sailing back to Gascony, in the company of the *Grand Marie*, *Little Marie* and *Thomas*. The ships ran into a fierce winter storm off the 'Foreland' of the Isle of Wight and could go no further. The *Little Trinity* was damaged, and had to put into Southampton for repairs, but the others went back to the Camber in order to take shelter. Within a few weeks, however, the Bordeaux voyage had been scrapped, and the ships were needed for a 'seakeeping' patrol.[108]

As Colin Richmond points out, 'seakeeping' or 'keeping the sea' was a long way from any modern idea of 'command of the sea'. Tactically, seakeeping patrols were offensive operations, with ships equipped to fight battles, but in strategic terms they were defensive. The patrols were supposed to repel enemy attacks at sea, defend the coast against invasion – or, at least, to give advance warning of attacks and invasions – and to inhibit piracy. Seakeeping fleets usually consisted of a number of royal ships, along with arrested and hired vessels. They carried retinues of men-at-arms and archers supplied under the normal system of military contracts or indentures (see plate 25). A seakeeping fleet would serve for a specified period, usually at least three months, and operations of this kind took place every year from 1415 to 1421.

The problem with such fleets, of course, was that any control they exerted was local and short-term. As events were to prove, the only ways to achieve long-term control of the English Channel were to destroy the naval power of the main enemy (France) and to occupy the French coastline.[109]

Orders for this first seakeeping patrol went out towards the end of January 1415. The fleet was eventually placed under the joint command of Gilbert, Lord Talbot and Sir Thomas Carew, and a commission to muster the force was issued on 26 January. The military contingent came to 150 men-at-arms and 300 archers, with a dozen ships. There were seven royal vessels, including the ships *Katherine* and *Thomas*, the balingers *Gabriel* and *Paul* and five privately owned ships from London, Bayonne, Winchelsea and Rye. The masters of all these vessels were empowered to press sailors into service.

The expedition lasted fifty days and finished on 11 April, when it put in at the Camber. Its stated aim was to resist the king's enemies at sea, who were planning to assemble 'great fleets of ships to invade the realm.' As is common with these seakeeping patrols, there is next to no information about what

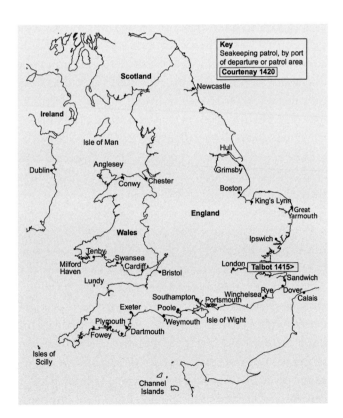

57 The departure point of the 1415 Talbot seakeeping patrol.

happened, though the force did capture five vessels. The prize ships were all Breton (despite a truce with Brittany), the merchant ship *St Gabriel de Hennebont* and four small crayers of between 30 and 40 tons, all apparently taken in the first half of March. The *St Gabriel* was taken to Southampton and rebuilt as the 40-ton royal balinger *Gabriel Harfleur*, while the crayers were laid up at Winchelsea and stayed there. Seizing and keeping these five ships was a stunning display of royal hypocrisy, in view of the Statute of Truces, especially as the Crown continued to remind English ports of the need to respect the Breton truce.[110]

By the time Talbot set sail, the king had fixed his mind on invading France. In February, the royal council came up with a naval defence scheme for the English coast 'during the king's voyage' – the invasion of France. The plans envisaged that the force would be deployed in three groups, on the south and east coasts, with two ships, five barges, five balingers and 1,040 sailors. The strongest group was to cover the area between Plymouth and the Isle of Wight, an interesting comment on what was perceived to be the most vulnerable stretch of coastline. In the event, the vessels were never deployed: even if they had been, the groups were too weak to do more than provide early warning of an invasion force.[111]

Nowadays, the 1415 invasion of Normandy, the capture of Harfleur and the battle of Agincourt are the most famous events of Henry's reign. This is mainly down to William Shakespeare. Agincourt, a victory against great odds in hostile territory, inevitably takes centre stage in the story. Henry's triumph delivered a shattering material and psychological blow to the French, and the king won great fame as a soldier. However, this military success relied on the ability of the English to cross the Channel, land an army in one piece and then take Harfleur. But, as Ian Mortimer and other historians have asked, why did Henry choose to land on an enemy coast and take Harfleur? The English already had possessions in what is now mainland France, the port and enclave of Calais in the north and the duchy of Aquitaine (Gascony) in the south-west. Both could have been seen as better jumping-off points for invasion.

Mortimer suggests that Henry chose Harfleur because it was not too far from England and offered the chance of a successful siege or battle that would both demonstrate God's favour and equal Edward III's feats (he had taken Calais in 1347). This is certainly possible, but there was also a pressing strategic need to capture the town. Along with Dieppe, Harfleur was one of the most significant ports for French pirates, privateers and raiders. The suppression of piracy and the defence of the south coast were compelling reasons for seizing Harfleur. Also, it stood at the mouth of the River Seine, with the French naval dockyard, the Clos des Galées, a few miles upstream at Rouen. Even though the dockyard was moribund by this date, the English could not ignore its potential to support a French fleet. Beyond Rouen, over 100 miles up the Seine, stood the French capital, Paris, a point unlikely to be lost on someone thinking about taking the French Crown.[112]

Shipping arrests for the Harfleur expedition were already under way by early February 1415, with vessels ordered to assemble at Southampton. The process of hiring Dutch transports was in train by April. On 19 March, the government had summoned the feudal shipping levy from the Cinque Ports, and on 18 May the Ports' vessels gathered at Dover to go to Holland and escort the Dutch ships back to England. Also on 19 March, a Bristol ropemaker named John Gibbe was commissioned to conscript workers to make ropes. The reason is not given, but as Gibbe was also told to supply canvas, the ropes were probably intended for the fleet.

The assembly date for the invasion fleet slipped in the months up to departure. To start with, it was 18 March; then, on 11 April, a decree went out for all shipping of 20 tons and more between Bristol and Newcastle to assemble by 8 May. The English ships were to gather at Southampton, and the foreign vessels at London, Sandwich or Winchelsea. On 27 May, the Sheriff of Hampshire was instructed, 'on pain of the king's grievous wrath', to make a proclamation that the people of Hampshire were to 'bake and brew' for the next three months to provide victuals for the invasion force. Between 3 May and 4 June, royal shipmasters were given warrants allowing them to press crews, and the large, 330-ton ship *Nicholas* joined the royal fleet in the Thames on 4 May. The nine royal vessels definitely known to have been used in the 1415 invasion were all sailing ships, though the rebuilt and patriotically renamed balinger *Gabriel Harfleur* may also have taken part. The sailing vessels were the great ship *Trinity Royal* and the ships *Grand Marie*, *Katherine*, *Nicholas*, *Little Marie*, *Little Trinity*, *Thomas*, *Philip* and *Rodcogge*. It was the last significant royal naval force ever to be composed entirely of one-masters.

The *Trinity Royal* was resplendent with heraldic imagery that proclaimed the king's status and piety (see Introduction), but flags and other symbols were also issued to various other royal ships. The *Nicholas* and *Katherine* were the second- and third-largest vessels, and, like the *Trinity Royal*, received decorated sail covers. The *Nicholas* sported the three ostrich plumes of the Prince of Wales, and the *Katherine* carried a cover displaying an antelope ascendant above a beacon. The sail covers could only be fully displayed when the ships were under full sail, and this may mean that these two ships were flotilla leaders, their size and decorated sails marking them out for other ships to follow.

Orders went out to both local officials and the Church to defend the country in the king's absence. Though the notion may sound odd in a medieval context, security was made as tight as possible. On 3 July, all ports from Bristol to Newcastle were told to prevent any foreigners from setting sail. On the day Henry boarded the *Trinity Royal*, 7 August, towns were ordered to keep watch until Halloween. Innkeepers were not to let any 'unknown stranger' stay more than a day and a night unless they declared

58 Portchester Castle: the keep and part of the royal apartments where Henry V stayed in 1415 before embarking in the *Trinity Royal* for France.

what their business happened to be. Anyone who refused to divulge what they were doing was to be slung in prison. There was perhaps a degree of 'spy mania' here, but the precautions worked. The first Frenchmen to know that the fleet had sailed were some Boulogne fishermen, who spotted it in the Channel.[113]

The fleet gathered at Southampton and along the south coast was very large. As I have said elsewhere in this book, I don't really believe the figures of 1,500 or 1,600 vessels bandied about by various chroniclers, but there certainly must have been hundreds of vessels. The army may have numbered up to 12,000 men, with supporting non-combatants – servants, craftsmen and the like – 'conservatively' estimated at 3,000. In addition to these men, there were large numbers of horses and considerable quantities of weapons, victuals and other supplies.

The fleet, large as it was, apparently did not have sufficient capacity for all the men and materiel it was supposed to move. Orders were sent out on 27 July for more ships, causing a delay. Matters were hindered further by the revelation of an alleged plot against Henry at Southampton, and the summary trial and execution of its leading figures. The fleet finally set sail on Sunday

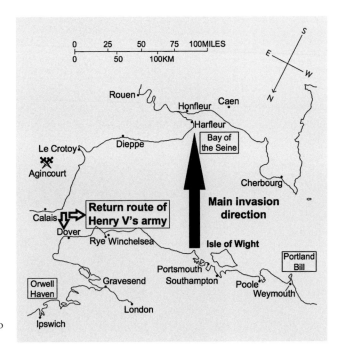

59 The campaign of Harfleur and Agincourt, 1415: the general routes to and from France.

11 August, though some men and materiel had to be left behind, as there were still not enough vessels.

The crossing took two days, and the force arrived off the Chef de Caux (modern Cap de la Hève), a few miles from Harfleur, at around 5 p.m. on Tuesday 13 August. Henry called a council of war aboard the *Trinity Royal*, and forbade anyone from landing before him. The only exception made was for a patrol led by the Earl of Huntingdon, which went ashore under cover of darkness to reconnoitre the countryside around the landing beach. The king himself landed between six and seven o'clock on the morning of Wednesday 14 August. This was two to two-and-a-half hours past high tide that day, with low tide at around 11.13 a.m. The king was followed by what was said to be the greater part of his army in 'little ships' [*naviculis*], boats and skiffs [*cimbis*]'.

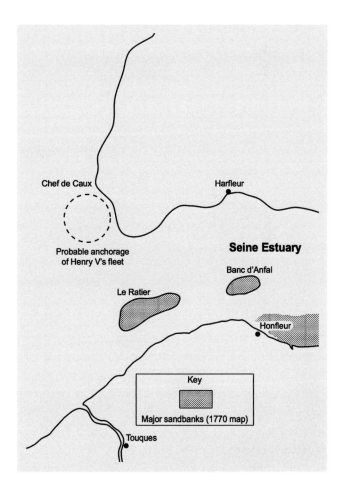

60 Conjectural map of the landing area, 1415.

It has been suggested by Hoskins and Curry that the landing beach was one about 1 mile south-east of Cap de la Hève, away from the cliffs and rocks around the point itself, and within the mouth of the Seine. A wide beach existed here in the eighteenth century, and perhaps before.[114] Unloading this armada is said to have taken three days, ending on 17 August, though this may have been quick for disembarking a medieval army. Men, horses, armour, weapons, stores and victuals all had to be transferred into small boats. The horses must have been the most difficult to unload, the poor creatures disoriented and jittery after the sea voyage, and then unloaded into a rocking boat via a block and tackle rigged on a yardarm.[115]

There is no information about the organisation of the fleet anchorage, but it is likely to have covered a very wide area. Modern charts show a roughly triangular 'shelf' of shallower water off the probable landing beach area, between roughly 3.5 and 6.5m deep at low water and around 6–9m at high water (the area now has the names Banc de l'Éclat and Petite Rade). It would have been crowded, and dangerous, with so many anchors laid out in a constricted space – anchoring over someone else's anchor could get your ship holed if the tide went out too far. The anchorage was also very exposed. Like the Allies on D-Day in 1944, Henry was lucky with his 'window' of good weather. One chronicler noted that the landing beach was very stony, with large and dangerous rocks. The prevailing winds in the Channel come from the west or south-west at that time of year, and a strong blow from those directions could have turned the landing beach into a lee shore, driving ships to destruction.[116]

Once ashore, Henry lost no time in laying siege to Harfleur. The port could not be attacked by water, because a heavy iron chain was stretched across its entrance, but English ships were still able to blockade the seaward side of the town, preventing any French vessels from getting in or out. Meanwhile, the crowd of ships at the invasion beach started to thin out. The Dutch ships left Normandy soon after the landing. Some of the English ships went on 12 September, after six weeks' service, according to a handful of surviving pay accounts. Enough remained, though, to maintain the blockade throughout the siege, which ended when Harfleur capitulated on 22 September.

In the aftermath of the siege, at least 1,693 English soldiers were invalided home from 28 September, suffering from dysentery, fever or wounds. Henry now had to decide what to do with the rest of his army. He left part of it as a garrison at Harfleur, and on 8 October took a road home across 120 miles of French countryside, to English-held Calais. The reasons behind this choice are a matter of speculation. It may be that the king did not think the risk too great, or that he sought a trial by battle in the field. It is also possible that there was not enough English shipping left in Harfleur to carry his army. Many ships had gone home by then, and some of those that remained were wrecked by a storm in early October. Perhaps Henry simply thought it would be easier to find a passage for thousands of men in the busy port of Calais, just 20 miles from Dover.[117]

The anti-invasion preparations of the French had been a case of too little, too late. Like the Germans occupying France in 1944, they knew that an invasion was coming, but had no real idea as to where and when it would take place. It does look as though Henry's security measures worked. The warning from the Boulogne fishermen was reported to Normandy, but nothing effective was done. French reinforcements were stuck at Rouen when Harfleur fell; thirteen balingers laid up in the Clos des Galées were refurbished, but were not ready for use until a month after Henry had landed.[118]

Eight of the royal ships were back in England by 17 October, at Sandwich and Winchelsea; the last to come home was the *Philip*, which returned to London on 1 November. In between these two dates, Henry fought and won the battle of Agincourt, on 25 October. The battle did not destroy French military power, but the death or capture of large numbers of men, including members of the aristocracy, dealt a heavy blow to France. Henry and his army marched on to Calais, and most returned home via Dover in November. The king himself crossed on 16 November, despite a storm that sank two of the ships in his company. It was said that Henry did not even suffer seasickness.[119]

The last four months of 1415 saw five vessels added to the royal fleet. These were: the ships *Margaret* (70 tons), *Marie Breton* (of unknown tonnage, but small) and *Grand Gabriel* (180 tons), the rebuilt balinger *Gabriel Harfleur* and finally, on 17 November, the great ship *Holy Ghost* (740 tons).[120] The *Gabriel Harfleur* may have been involved in the Normandy campaign, and its new name certainly celebrated Henry's triumph. Construction of a third great ship began in about September 1415, at Smallhythe in Kent, and a master shipwright named William Goodey was paid for his work on the project from 6 October. Although the new vessel did not yet have a name, it would be the 1,000-ton *Jesus*.[121]

Christmas saw most of the royal ships in harbour, apart from the *Margaret*, which sailed into Chester on 27 December with 60 tons of wine aboard. The year had seen Henry use a combination of English and Dutch sea power to mount the most successful invasion of France since the 1340s, followed by a victory in the field that made his military reputation easily the equal of that of his predecessor, Edward III. The royal fleet now stood at fifteen vessels, fourteen sailing ships and a solitary balinger, not counting 'followers' and great boats. However, despite the successful invasion of Normandy, Henry's naval forces had yet to see any serious fighting. That would all change in 1416.

7

THE BLOODY SEA-ROAD TO CONQUEST, 1416–18

In Ian Mortimer's words, 1415 was Henry V's 'year of glory'. That's certainly how Shakespeare saw it, because his narrative slips from the end of the battle of Agincourt to the negotiations for the Treaty of Troyes in 1420. History minus 'the boring stuff', perhaps, but also history without 'some of the really important stuff'. Henry had captured one French town and won a great battle that had decided nothing. Then he went home. As the historian Anne Curry wrote, the question facing Henry was: 'After Agincourt, what next?'[122] The spring and summer of 1416 saw the triumphs of 1415 seemingly turn to ashes as Harfleur was blockaded, the French built up their sea power and England suffered attack.

But the English authorities were not fearful at the start of 1416. In early January, eight royal ships once again set off for Bordeaux, and did not return until 21–22 May. They probably also served as convoy escorts, but sending half the royal fleet to Gascony was hardly the act of a government living in terror of French retribution in home waters. The same could be said of the dispatch of the *Little Trinity* to Prussia on 18 March.[123]

The Earl of Dorset, the Admiral of England, was confirmed as captain of the garrison at Harfleur in January 1416. He sailed to take up the post on 27 January, transported by a flotilla that comprised the *Trinity Royal* and *Holy Ghost*, with the balingers *Gabriel Harfleur*, *George* and *Little John*. The two great ships carried around 200 men each, many of them probably pressed into service. The *George* I and *Little John* were new to the king's ships, though the *George* was soon assigned to the defence of Harfleur, and ceased to be William Catton's concern.[124]

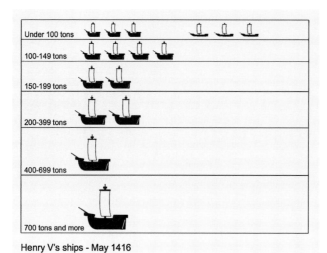

61 Operational vessels in the royal fleet, May 1416.

Henry V's ships - May 1416

The French, in the meantime, were looking to create a navy. Negotiations at Genoa in late 1415 and early 1416 led to the hire of a powerful force of eight galleys and nine war carracks, under the command of Giovanni di Grimaldi. According to W.L. Wylie, the warships left Genoa in late April, but other evidence (below) shows that they were already off western France or Brittany soon after Easter (19 April 1416). Each carrack was said to carry 100 crossbowmen, and one, the *Montagna Nigra* or *Black Mountain*, had 200. The Genoese ships were joined en route to France by sixty vessels from northern Spain, lent by the King of Castile.[125]

The first encounter between the English and the Genoese took place in late April, and it went badly for the English. An English merchant convoy left Bordeaux shortly after Easter, but prior to their departure, the English merchants, masters and mariners followed an old custom and elected an admiral for their convoy. The admiral they appointed was a Hull merchant named John Tutbury, owner of the ship *Christopher*. The men also swore a legal oath before the Constable of Bordeaux to the effect that they would stay together for mutual protection until they reached England. As it was heading home, the convoy ran into the Genoese carracks. The *Christopher* was a big ship, of at least 200 tons. It went into battle and allegedly saved a royal vessel described as 'the Great Hull of Brittany'. This was possibly the 210-ton *Katherine*, which had been bought in Brittany: it got back to England from a Bordeaux voyage on 22 May. However, the *Christopher* was taken and, according to the furious Tutbury, the other English ships ran away, 'to the disgrace of the English navy'. Tutbury took his complaints to both the 1416 Parliaments, and received government permission to buy back the ship and its cargo from the Genoese. He was able to do this somehow, and took the vessel back to Hull. It was a bad year for Tutbury, because one of his balingers was captured by the French while on a mission to resupply Harfleur.[126]

The 'disgrace' was not without cost to the Genoese because their commander, Grimaldi, was killed in the action. This may have adversely affected the performance of the Genoese galleys later in the summer, but for the time being the force just carried on its way. The ships made for the new French base of operations at Honfleur, just across the Seine Estuary from Harfleur. In the interim, the French had put together their own force of twelve royal galleys and 100 cogs, under the command of Guillaume de Montenay. Once the Genoese and Spanish vessels had arrived, the French may have had a fleet of close on 200 vessels, or perhaps more.

A French blockade of Harfleur was in place by early April, later reinforced by the arrival of the Genoese and Spanish in May. The English garrison was already in a difficult straits, because of losses suffered in an ill-judged land raid. All the Earl of Dorset had in the way of naval defence was an inadequate miniature navy with two small balingers. The blockade cannot have been too tight at the start, though, because Dorset was able to send envoys to England, warning that he would have to evacuate the port without fresh supplies. He also asked for a force of twenty-six vessels to patrol the mouth of the Seine and secure his supply lines. No flotilla was sent. There was a short Anglo–French truce at Harfleur from 5 May to 2 June 1416, which may have allowed some supplies in – the English government did attempt to revictual the port around this time. However, by 5 June Harfleur was under siege and blockade again, cut off and in an increasingly bad way.[127]

The French became much more belligerent at sea between March and July 1416. England, or at least Henry's government, began to shows signs of apprehension. A couple of sergeants-at-arms were sent out around 18 March to start arresting all ships and vessels of 20 tons or more between Bristol and Newcastle, with orders to send them to Orwell Haven on the Suffolk–Essex border. The plan was to concentrate the nation's ships in this large estuary so that they could be protected. The reason given for this move was intelligence that the French and their Genoese allies and others were planning to attack various English ports and destroy the ships there. The 'Orwell order' was restated in a letter that went to all coastal counties from the West Country to Northumberland on 5 April, which also decreed that warning beacons should be set up. Building beacons was a sensible precaution, but the 'Orwell order' reeked of panic. However, there is not much evidence that anyone really obeyed it. Even the government itself was not consistent, as on 7 April the Constable of Dover Castle was told to conscript ships for the passage of the Holy Roman Emperor from Calais, and on 12 April William Soper was ordered to arrest vessels in Southampton.[128]

Given the timing of the first of the 'Orwell arrests', the king must have got word of the Genoese and Spanish reinforcements by mid-March, though the French started taking the initiative at sea even before their allies turned up. The *Gesta Henrici Quinti* says that they sent a strong force to try to burn the royal ships at Southampton, but only managed to destroy a few vessels; certainly, none of the royal ships were damaged at this time. They also attacked various other places along the coast, including the Isle of Portland, which they burned, although most of the local population was evacuated before the attack. The *Gesta* speaks of 'manly' resistance against the raiders, but does not offer any more details.

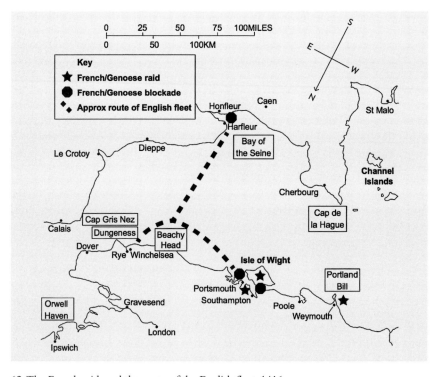

62 The French raids and the route of the English fleet, 1416.

Things got worse. By early May there were French blockades off Portsmouth and Southampton; they also made an attack on Portsmouth and a landing on the Isle of Wight, burning and looting as they went. The Genoese played a part in these operations, though they lost a carrack when it ran aground. The crew managed to escape with their loot and the remaining French vessels made their way home.

The fear of coastal raids and worse led to the issue of commissions of array from 14 to 29 May, sent to the Isle of Wight, Dorset, Hampshire, Wiltshire, Surrey, Sussex and Berkshire. The commissions warned that more French and Genoese attacks were imminent, and issued orders for local troops to be raised. The directive to prepare fire beacons was also repeated.

The precise chronology of the French raids is not clear, though there seems to have been a second phase of attacks on the Isle of Wight between mid-June and mid-July. This failed because a storm blew the raiders back across the Channel. The extent of the French raids and blockades was both worrying and dangerous for the English. It highlighted the vulnerability of ports like Southampton and Portsmouth, and the apparent impotence of the English naval forces. As the French historian Charles de La Roncière remarked, 'the weather had protected England better than its fleets.'[129]

The French raids took place during the visit of Sigismund, the Holy Roman Emperor, to England. Amongst other things, Sigismund was trying a mediate a peace settlement between England and France, and it's possible that the raids were intended by the French Armagnac faction to torpedo any negotiations. It seems unlikely, however, that by this stage Henry envisaged anything other than a 'military solution' to his dealings with France. The day before the Emperor landed, a contract was made with the Earl of Huntingdon, Sir Edward Courtenay and John, Lord Clifford to take a force of 893 men-at-arms and 1,800 archers to sea for three months. Its purpose was 'for safekeeping the sea and defending the kingdom of England'. Huntingdon was overall commander and the ships were mustered at Hull, Winchelsea, Southampton, Plymouth and other ports.

There are other, smaller signs of the move towards renewed conflict. Timber for building a *somercastell* in the great ship *Holy Ghost* was being carted to Southampton as early as April 1416, and both this vessel and the *Trinity Royal* received extra superstructures in May and June. This was preparation for battle. The great ships were assigned to Huntingdon's force, once again crewed by 200 sailors each; five large Prussian vessels, totalling 1,600 tons of shipping, were also hired for the expedition.

Huntingdon's orders, issued on 12 May, say a lot about the strategic situation at the time and the delicate diplomatic balance Henry was trying to maintain. The earl was forbidden to attack ships and people from a list of countries that included Portugal, Denmark, Sweden, Norway, Holland, Prussia, Castile and Flanders – the last thing Henry needed was a new enemy. Once the fleet was ready, Huntingdon was to go to Harfleur as quickly as possible and relieve the garrison, something that could only be done by breaking the blockade. After that was achieved, Huntingdon's force would head south and conduct a seakeeping patrol.[130]

The king briefly took over command of the expedition from Huntingdon, but soon had to relinquish it to his brother, John, Duke of Bedford because the Emperor and diplomacy claimed Henry's attention. Bedford was appointed commander on 22 July, again for a period of three months. The exact size of the fleet is uncertain, but it had been gathered from a large number of English ports. Only a handful of royal ships are definitely known to have been involved. These were the great ships (the *Holy Ghost* was Bedford's flagship – see plates 17c and 18c) and the balingers *James* and *Little John*.

Cannon, gunpowder, gunstones, lances, bows, arrows and bowstrings and other items were bought for the voyage. A payment made on 18 July refers to ships for the expedition being kept at London 'on account of the fear of enemies gathering outside the port of Southampton' though the enemy had gone by the time the disparate western and northern fleets had concentrated at Southampton and in the Camber by Winchelsea in late July or early August.[131]

The raids and blockades staged by the French and Genoese had delayed the Harfleur relief expedition by two or three months, and put the English on the defensive. It was a very effective use of sea power, but the effort could not be maintained indefinitely. The two sections of Bedford's fleet finally set sail in early August. According to the writer of the *Gesta*, contrary winds at first drove the ships all over the place, but eventually, using the tidal currents in the Channel, the force came together off Beachy Head. The wind changed on Friday 14 August and the fleet was able to sail at some speed for France. Bedford reached the mouth of the Seine that evening. His force dropped anchor, and small oared vessels – probably balingers – were sent out to locate the enemy.[132]

English prisoners had already told the French that a relief force was coming, and there was high tension in their fleet on the night of the 14–15th. The commander of this force, Guillaume II, Vicomte de Narbonne, had his men stand to arms through the hours of darkness, which cannot have helped

63 Part of the Normandy coast. (Denis, 1770)

64 The Bay of the Seine, detail: Harfleur had retreated from the sea by the late eighteenth century due to silting, a retreat that has continued into modern times, and Le Havre was not established until 1517, but the map still gives a good sense of the general lie of the land. (Denis, 1770)

119

their battle readiness the next day. The Spanish ships, the Genoese galleys and some French balingers apparently retreated to Honfleur and played no part in the battle. A well-informed French chronicler, the monk of St Denys, says that when the English fleet dropped anchor at sunset the Spanish saw the enemy, lost their nerve and fled, taking their sixty ships with them (this is also recorded by the Venetian chronicler Morosini). The Spanish later claimed that they were only provided with fishing vessels, craft too weak for battle. If this was the case, one wonders why they were sent in the first place. The loss of the Genoese galleys may have been a bigger blow, perhaps a consequence of the death of Grimaldi in the spring.

The St Denys chronicler has Narbonne giving a 'victory or death' speech to stiffen the resolve of his remaining captains, particularly the Genoese, who had been rattled by the departure of the Spanish. The Genoese stayed put, however, despite passing a stormy, fearful and tiring night.

The naval battle of Harfleur was fought the next day, Saturday 15 August. This, one of the most important sea battles of the Hundred Years War, is difficult to describe or even locate accurately. The map (plate 66) is an attempt to understand both the nature of its setting and something of the course of events. The positions of the coastline around Harfleur and the sandbanks are based on the evidence of maps and charts ranging in date from the fifteenth to the eighteenth century. This inevitably involves a lot of conjecture, though the existence of sandbanks between Harfleur and Honfleur in 1416 seems pretty likely, as a ship fleeing to Honfleur after the battle was wrecked on a sandbar. This is important, because it confirms that the action was confined to the northern side of the estuary.[133]

The two fixed locations in the battle were Harfleur and Honfleur, where the ships of the French and their allies were based. They are almost directly opposite each other, and Harfleur stood either on the estuary in 1416, or close to it, though later silting turned it into an inland town. The French blockade of the port must have covered both the harbour mouth and an area to the west, to prevent English ships from getting in. This gives a rough starting position for the French on the eve of battle.

A coastal pilot book of 1825 warns anyone trying to reach Le Havre or Rouen that they should not attempt it without a pilot to guide them in, and notes that between Le Havre and Honfleur there 'are several banks, some of which shift'. Le Havre did not exist until 1517, but the later entrance to port comes out in the general area where Henry's army landed in 1415. This was described as the 'Little Road' in the 1825 pilot, about 1.5 miles south-south-west of Cap de la Hève (Chef de Caux), and it was probably where Bedford's fleet anchored on 14 August 1416 (the 1588 *Mariners Mirrour* and a seventeenth-century chart mark an anchorage in this area).

The *Gesta* says that the opposing fleets started to move towards each other in the early dawn, suggesting that the wind offered some help to both sides. Daybreak would have been between five and six, with low tide at around 9.10 a.m. The direction of the falling tide and the outfall from the Seine would have helped impel the Franco-Genoese fleet, though the force of these currents would have weakened as low tide approached. It was perhaps no coincidence that the action was said to have started around 9 a.m. The falling tide may actually have made things a bit safer for the English – the 1825 pilot book warns that the fast current running into the Seine on a rising tide could drive a ship ashore.

The numbers of vessels given for the opposing fleets in various sources are impossible to check, and we don't have any figures from administrative documents. According to a letter of 23 August 1416, written in Bruges and sent to Venice, the French started with 100 ships with castles, besides eight Genoese carracks and a dozen galleys. However, after the retreat of the Spanish and others, the force available to Narbonne on the morning of the 15 August may have numbered as few as thirty-eight craft. A Venetian letter claims that Bedford's fleet had 300 vessels, big and small. The monk of St Denys, a credible French chronicler, gives a figure of 250 for Bedford's fleet.

65 Ship's trumpeters, after a fifteenth-century manuscript. (Nicolas 1847, p.386)

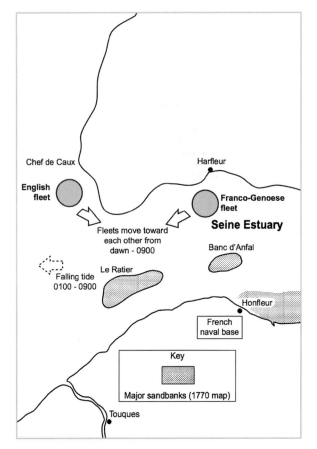

66 The setting and the possible opening phase of the battle of Harfleur. The coastline around Harfleur is a reconstruction based on fifteenth to eighteenth-century maps and charts, as are the sandbanks. The positions of the two fleets are conjectural. The battle area is probably now covered by land, and perhaps only the discovery of large concentrations of arrowheads and other projectiles could localise the site of the action.

The St Denys chronicle says that Narbonne, seeing that the weather had calmed down at daybreak, used the trumpets and clarions of the French heralds to sound an order for his ships to advance. They were in tight formation, to give them greater advantage in the battle. The chronicler claims that the English only raised their anchors when they saw the French force begin to move, though other sources say the English took the initiative. Whichever side got going first, light winds meant that it took the fleets three or possibly four hours to crawl close enough together to begin fighting.

It is possible that the English swung to the south and then round to the north 'to outflank the serried squadron of the French', as Wylie puts it, but we don't know. What is likely is that the commanders of individual vessels did their best to ensure that they grappled with ships of roughly equivalent size, to avoid being overwhelmed. This means that the *Trinity Royal* and *Holy Ghost* would have gone for the great Genoese carracks.

The battle must have begun with exchanges of arrows, crossbow bolts and gunstones as the ships closed the range, but it was decided by a series of ferocious boarding actions. These were fought with the aid of projectile weapons, as well as the swords, axes and lances in the hands of the men-at-arms. St Denys makes special mention of stones and heavy iron gads thrown from the topcastles of the Genoese carracks, 'which caused much havoc among the enemy'. He also writes of the English using iron hooks and grapnels to latch on to their opponents. They attempted to board and destroy their masts and rigging, but were said to have been driven off 'twenty times' by blows from lances and other weapons. St Denys got his account from eyewitnesses, the French royal heralds, who were present at the battle. They spoke of ships manoeuvring, trying to attack the sides of enemy vessels, then going bow-to-bow, boarding over the prow. The heralds particularly commended the courage of the Genoese crossbowmen, who fought hard, and may well have died to a man.

The prosaic language of the administrative accounts for Henry's ships provides a revealing and dramatic footnote to the story of this battle. The only two English ships for which there is specific evidence of battle damage are the *Holy Ghost* and the *Trinity Royal*, and this is recorded in their inventories. The tables summarise these:

Holy Ghost – items lost or destroyed in battle, 'lost and sunk in the sea', 1416[134]

Standing rigging	Yard	Sail	Ground tackle★	Other gear
17 ropes	8 ropes	10 ropes	1 anchor	1 hook rope
			5 cables	2 cranelines
			2 buoy ropes	1 grapnel with a 12-fathom chain

Trinity Royal – items lost or destroyed in battle, 1416

Standing rigging	Yard	Sail	Ground tackle★	Other gear
1 rope	1 sail	1 sail	4 cables	1 great lantern
4 pulleys	yard	bonnet	6 hawsers	2 lanterns
			2 buoys	3 sounding leads
				1 seizing grapnel

★anchors, cables and buoy ropes

Certain things can be deduced about the nature of the fighting from this evidence (see plate 15c). The three leads lost by the *Trinity Royal* point to frantic attempts to sound the water as the English fleet approached the enemy. Both great ships lost grapnels in this battle, bearing out what St Denys says about ships grappling and then being forced away. The missing anchor and other ground tackle suggest that both vessels anchored at some point in the battle, or perhaps even cut their anchor cables in order to get under way. It's also quite possible that they used cables and hawsers to secure themselves to their opponents.

The huge amount of rigging destroyed in the *Holy Ghost*, and the sail yard missing from the *Trinity Royal*, show that boarders got on to both ships and tried to immobilise them by wrecking their rigging. In the case of the *Holy Ghost*, the Genoese or French came close to bringing down the mainmast. The diagram (plate 15c) shows just part of the head ropes missing, but it may be that they were all cut away on one side of the mast.

Both great ships went into battle with large complements of men-at-arms and archers, as well as 400 sailors and boys, so it is impossible to know how many weapons were used up on the two vessels in this battle. The *Trinity Royal* may also have carried a weapon called a 'shearhook', a large blade used to cut the sails and rigging of an enemy ship and mounted on a yardarm for this purpose.

The fighting lasted for hours, perhaps into the evening. Whatever its duration, the carnage ended with an English victory. The *Gesta* claims that the French and Genoese lost 1,500 dead and 400 taken prisoner, with nearly 100 dead on the English side. St Denys says that Bedford was wounded, along with 700 knights and squires. Such casualty figures are unverifiable, and all of the chronicles had their biases. The Venetian chronicler Morosini, who had less of an axe to grind, merely says that many were killed on both sides. The English captured three carracks, belonging to Opecchino Lomellino, Ilario Imperiali and Simone Pinelli. According to Morosini, the Genoese crews were all killed. It seems that other prize vessels were taken, though only the three carracks ended up as part of the English royal fleet; four other carracks escaped. A large Flemish or German hulk (a type of big ship), called the *Black Hulk* of Flanders in some sources, is said to have gone down, but this might have been confused with the Genoese carrack *Montagna Nigra*.

After the battle, Bedford sent part of his fleet home with the wounded; the rest of the force made for Harfleur, for the victory had broken the blockade. French oared craft subsequently tried to attack the English fleet with incendiaries, but failed. The courageous and tenacious Genoese had suffered badly, and their fortunes did not improve after the battle. The carrack of the Genoese commander, Giovanni Spinola, was caught on a sandbank the next day and wrecked. Following this, the remaining Genoese vessels returned home, for fear that the English might attack Honfleur.

Some of the English ships stayed close to Harfleur for some time after the battle, for a letter (plates 17c and 18c) shows that the *Holy Ghost* was off the Chef de Caux on 28 August. News of the victory had reached Henry V on 21 August, when he was at Smallhythe in Kent inspecting the construction of his new great ship, the *Jesus*. He had just signed a treaty with the Holy Roman Emperor, and both of them attended a service in Canterbury Cathedral to give thanks for Bedford's success and for what was seen as God's hand in the battle.

The scene in the Seine Estuary was less holy. Floating corpses were visible for several days after the battle, driven backwards and forwards by the tide. Even in the fifteenth century, not everyone was carried away by the martial spirit, for St Denys commented that it was 'deplorable that so many Christians should be sacrificed in the vain desire to acquire glory'.[135]

The stories of ordinary soldiers of the Hundred Years War have seldom survived. Thomas Hostell's brief account of his experiences is one of those rare survivals. He served both Henry IV and Henry V as a man-at-arms, on land and at sea, and outlined his record of service in a petition to Henry VI, made in the early years of the young king's reign (the petition was published in the nineteenth century, and part of it is reproduced here with modernised spelling). The document is written in the third person, probably by a notary employed by Hostell, but still gives some sense of the sheer violence of battle in Henry V's time. Half-blinded and disfigured by a springald bolt at the siege of Harfleur, Hostell soldiered on, fighting at Agincourt:

> and at the taking of the carracks on the sea, therewith a gad of iron his plates smitten into his body and his hand smitten in sunder, and sore hurt, maimed and wounded, by mean(s) whereof he being sore feebled and debruised, now fall to great age and poverty, greatly indebted, and may not help himself, having not wherewith to be sustained nor relieved, but of men's gracious alms, and being for his said service never yet recompensed nor rewarded ...

It's not clear if Hostell was referring to the 1416 or the 1417 carrack battle, but his account graphically illustrates the horrific wounds caused by an iron gad that found a human target. The weapon hit his plate armour so hard that it drove part of it into his body, and tore his hand apart. The one-eyed, maimed old soldier was reduced to living on charity, but we do not know if his plea for help was ever answered.[136]

The 15 August battle soon became known as the 'Battle of Harfleur'. William Catton's administrative account merely describes it as a 'voyage in the company of the Duke of Bedford for the capture of diverse carracks on the sea in the 4th year [of Henry V's reign]'. If Catton was a poet, he hid it well, but his officialese emphasises just how much the English saw the Genoese carracks as the main threat to them in the Channel. And now Henry had three of them, soon bearing new names that combined the religious and the patriotic: *George*, *Marie Hampton* and *Marie Sandwich*. The English now also knew that they could defeat the carracks in battle. The balance of sea power in the Channel was beginning to shift in their direction.[137]

1416–17: Getting Ready for the Second Invasion

The 1416 victory made it possible for Henry to think seriously about a second invasion of France, though the sea war itself was far from over.[138] Henry had to cross to Calais on 4 September for important negotiations with the Emperor (who had gone ahead) and the Duke of Burgundy. However, he was informed that a substantial fleet of the French and their allies was massing at sea 'to hinder his passage'. In the end, sixty ships were conscripted for Henry's voyage from Sandwich to Calais, though it took about a day to complete this short journey, and the English fleet had to use tidal currents and oars in order to make headway.[139]

The English naval build-up continued: on 4 September an order went to Bayonne to build two ships for the king, and six days later the three captured carracks officially joined the royal fleet. Two balingers entered service on 18 and 21 September, the new two-master *George* (120 tons) and the *Craccher* (56 tons) respectively. The *George* was soon at sea and was used to bring Henry safely back from Calais to Dover through a bad storm. Not everyone was enjoying the afterglow of victory at Harfleur, though, as the authorities were on the lookout to arrest men and ships that had deserted from Bedford's fleet after the battle.[140]

In late September, a Genoese carrack was unsuccessfully pursued and attacked by six English balingers from Calais, a minor action with much aristocratic derring-do, but of no strategic significance (see Chapter 5). Work on expanding the royal fleet continued: on 22 October 1416, the 120-ton royal balinger *Anne* was floated from its dock at Southampton. Just over a week later, the building account for the great ship *Grace Dieu* began officially, although work of some kind had already started at Southampton in the summer. The same month saw the English Parliament complaining for the second time that year about the non-payment of tontight money. Despite bland assurances that the payments would be forthcoming, the situation may have led some shipowners to evade royal service if they could.[141]

There was a truce between England and France from 9 October 1416 to 14 February 1417, but this did not stop the government from making it clear in the autumn Parliament that Henry was going to invade France again.[142] January and February 1417 saw preparations for both a seakeeping voyage and a (not very) mysterious-sounding voyage 'by the king in his own person to foreign parts'.

The seakeeping voyage involved three units, one at Dartmouth, led by Sir Thomas Carew, and two at Winchelsea under Sir John Mortimer and a Gascon lord, Pons de Castelhon. The force carried 616 men-at-arms, 1,232 archers and over 800 mariners, the equivalent of the adult male population of a moderately large town. Six royal ships took part, including the recently captured carracks *Marie Hampton* and *Marie Sandwich*, along with ten other English vessels, two Venetian carracks, three big ships from Gdansk and one from Holland. Nine of the twenty-two vessels were barges and balingers, but it was far and away the most powerful seakeeping force England had yet sent out. The squadrons were mustered in their respective assembly ports on 1 March. They were directed, at least in theory, against a wide range of enemies – the French, the Bretons, the Spanish and the Genoese.

The conditions imposed on Carew and his men were fairly standard ones for war voyages. His force was not to capture any foreign ships from places that had a truce with England, or any vessels with safe conducts from the king. A quarter of all prize ships and goods would belong to the king, with a 'reasonable' split of the proceeds from the ransoms of any 'great captains' taken prisoner.

Physical conditions on such ships must have been congested and grim. The voyage lasted six months, and the ships were not supposed to go into port unless driven there by bad weather. Even then, the only men who could go ashore were those sent for victuals, and once the weather cleared, the ships had to put to sea again.[143] The two groups seem to have operated independently, probably covering the eastern and western halves of the English Channel. Carew's ships returned to Dartmouth on 30 August, as per his contract.

Seakeeping patrols were mounted in the English Channel every year from 1415 to 1421, the first time anyone had ever really tried to 'police' this sea area. They were not cheap. The wages bill for the 1417 patrol alone would have funded the construction of four *Grace Dieus*. The stated aims of these voyages were to 'keep' (i.e. patrol) the sea and defend the realm, but it is not easy to judge how successful they were. It is possible that seakeeping did inhibit pirates and smaller-scale naval activity just because it was known that a force of English ships was at sea. A report in early May 1417, for example, said that the seakeeping patrol had blocked the 'strait', presumably the Dover Strait. The patrols may also have provided reassurance to Henry and his commanders in England and France that they would have adequate warning of a major enemy raid or war fleet. Given how difficult it was to even spot, let alone intercept, an enemy force at sea, any such reassurance was rather illusory.[144]

The preparations for the 1417 invasion were under way before Carew and the others left harbour. Mounting a large seakeeping voyage and a cross-Channel invasion in the same year must have put a severe strain on England's shipping resources. Once again, additional ships were hired from Holland and Zeeland. They started coming into service from February: there were at least 116 of them, and probably more.[145] A new round of ship arrests started in England between March and May 1417, with Southampton as the assembly port, though as in 1415, the dates for assembling the fleet there kept slipping; the Cinque Ports' feudal levy was also called out. The royal fleet also grew, with the balingers *Swan*, *James* and *Nicholas* coming into service.[146]

The French hired more Genoese carracks in the winter of 1417. One two-masted carrack was actually captured in Southampton Water on about 7 March, though it is not clear if this was one of the newly recruited vessels or an off-course merchantman. Taken into the royal fleet and renamed the *Agase*, a serious attempt was made to refurbish it, but the carrack was later wrecked by a summer storm.[147]

The two great ships and the third of the seaworthy carracks were manned in March, though there are indications of manpower problems. In previous years, the *Trinity Royal* and *Holy Ghost* had carried crews of around 200 each: now they had only 130 and 100 respectively; the *George* received its specified complement of 100 sailors, however.

1c Henry V (1386–1422), by an unknown later artist, a portrait that derives ultimately from a lost medieval original. (Society of Antiquaries of London - LDSAL 296; Scharf XV, acquired by the Society before 1770)

2c Fourteenth/fifteenth-century gun loop in the citadel, St Malo, Brittany. Coastal raiding affected England, France and Brittany.

3c Amberley Castle in West Sussex was a manor house of the bishops of Chichester, and stands some 10 miles from the coast, on the River Arun. Despite its inland location, it was fortified in the 1370s because of the fear of French raids.

4c Rye, East Sussex: looking towards the sea, with the medieval Ypres Tower in the middle ground. Rye was one of the Cinque Ports that contributed men and ships to Henry V's fleets.

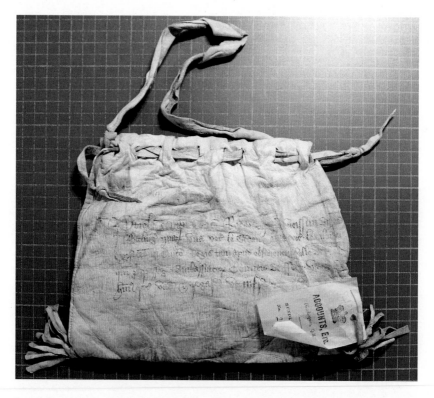

5c Medieval leather bag containing the wage accounts of Richard Rowe for the balingers *Swan* and *Valentine*. (TNA E101/49/27, The National Archives, Kew)

6c (*Above left*) 'Into thy hands I commend my spirit … ' (Psalm 31:5): detail of a figure of St Jude on the fifteenth-century rood screen of St Mary's, North Elmham, Norfolk. St Jude was one of the patron saints of seafarers though, oddly, ships were seldom named after him.

7c (*Above right*) Two figureheads on the fifteenth-century Mataro Model, depicting a human head and an animal. (© Ian Friel 1980)

8c (*Right*) 'A ship of forecastle': the fifteenth-century Mataro Model. (© Ian Friel 1980, photographed before modern conservation)

9c Detail of the fifteenth-century Mataro Model, showing the aftercastle. The small raised structure at the stern is a form of summercastle. (© Ian Friel 1980)

10c *(Below)* A reconstruction of the *Grace Dieu* anchor (buoy rope ring omitted): the anchor stock is based on one from the *Mary Rose* (sunk 1545).

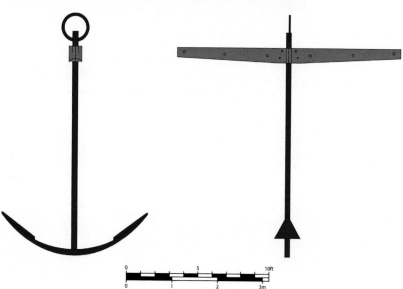

11c (*Opposite top*) A small boat and ship, from a fifteenth-century mural in the church of St Peter, Shorwell, Isle of Wight.

12c (*Opposite bottom*) One of the treasures of the world: the fifteenth-century Mataro Model. Dated scientifically to *c*. 1456–82, this very rare medieval ship model came from Catalonia and was clearly the work of a shipwright. Though sometimes described as a *nao* (Spanish for 'ship'), this skeleton-built model represents what the fifteenth-century English would have called a 'carrack'.[77] (Courtesy of the Maritiem Museum 'Prins Hendrik', Rotterdam, © Ian Friel 1980)

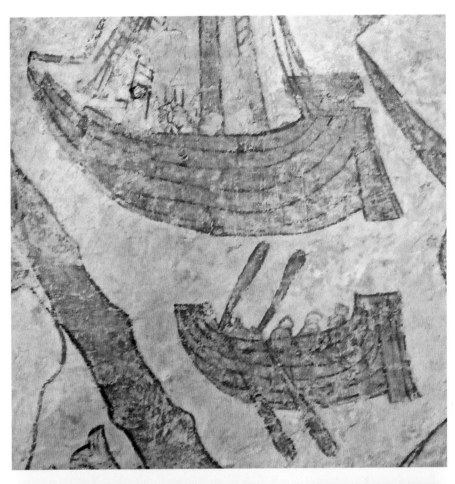

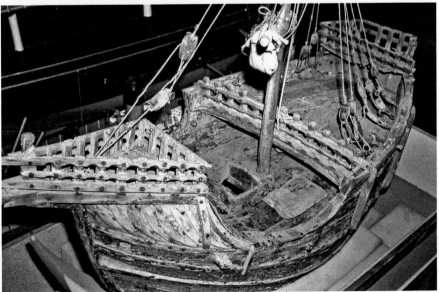

13c Fifteenth-century carving of St Jude, Holy Trinity church, Blythburgh, Suffolk. The boat the saint is holding is not a balinger, but it does have oar ports.

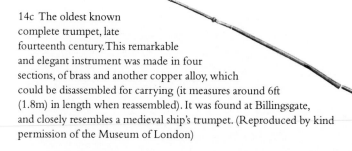

14c The oldest known complete trumpet, late fourteenth century. This remarkable and elegant instrument was made in four sections, of brass and another copper alloy, which could be disassembled for carrying (it measures around 6ft (1.8m) in length when reassembled). It was found at Billingsgate, and closely resembles a medieval ship's trumpet. (Reproduced by kind permission of the Museum of London)

15c The *Holy Ghost* and the battle of Harfleur, 1416. Items in red were lost by the ship (the hull and details of the rig are approximations). Not all of the losses are shown, but the attack on the rigging suggests a concerted attempt to immobilise the ship.

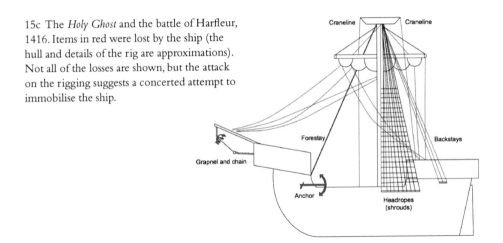

16c Carving of a two-masted ship, *c.* 1419. This bench or stall end was made for St Nicholas' chapel, Kings Lynn, and is dated by the style of its woodwork (the chapel was also rebuilt *c.* 1400–19). This extraordinary image offers a well-proportioned side view of a two-master shaped like a carrack, and its credible detail suggests that it was the work of someone very familiar with ships. The image's apparent closeness in date to the capture of the Genoese carracks in 1416 and 1417 raises the possibility that the carving was inspired by these victories, though the image could probably stand just as well as an image of one of Henry V's great ships as of a carrack. (Victoria and Albert Museum, W.16-1921)

17c The '*Holigost* Letter'. This Norman-French document gave Sir Walter Hungerford and John Skilling Esq. licence to leave the fleet in France and go home to convalesce from their illnesses. The licence was granted by John, Duke of Bedford, the fleet commander, 'in the ship called the *Holigost* on the River of Seine before *Kydecaux* [Chef de Caux]', 28 August 1416. Written in the battered *Holy Ghost* just under two weeks after the battle, this may also be the only surviving letter known to have been composed on one of Henry V's ships. (Wiltshire and Swindon Archives, Earl of Radnor MS 490/1547)

18c Seal of the Duke of Bedford from the '*Holigost* Letter'. John of Lancaster, Duke of Bedford (1389–1435) was one of Henry's younger brothers. He served as regent of France for most of the period between 1422 and his death, showing considerable political and military skill, though he also oversaw the trial and execution of Joan of Arc. (Wiltshire and Swindon Archives, Earl of Radnor MS 490/1547)

19c The Round Tower still stands at the mouth of Portsmouth Harbour. Though much altered over time, it is one of the few structures known to survive from Henry's naval war (photograph taken before the construction of the Spinnaker Tower).

20c The *Grace Dieu* site at low tide, early 1980s: the archaeologist on the left stands on the stern end of the keel; the bow end is slightly off-camera to the right. When the ship was intact, it would have blotted out most of this view.

English privateering seems to have carried on through the war, though the details are sketchy. There was, for example, a report in the spring of 1417 that Bristol privateers had captured enemy ships and cargoes and taken them into Southampton. Also, that spring, there were worries that indiscriminate ballast dumping by ships was starting to block up the vital anchorage at the Camber, and a commission was set up to find and designate safe dumping areas.[148]

The French were able to field a new, strong naval force by the summer, with nine Genoese carracks and other vessels. They don't seem to have tried a repeat of the raids on the English coast, but from April onwards they blockaded Harfleur once again. The English knew about the blockade and the Genoese reinforcements – amongst other things, between late May and late June the new balinger *Nicholas* was at sea 'towards foreign parts', obviously on a reconnaissance mission. Henry clearly understood that his invasion fleet could not sail until the naval opposition was removed, because he sent out the Earl of Huntingdon with a force to do just that.[149]

Huntingdon's expedition left port about the end of June. The royal vessels definitely known to have been in the fleet were the great ships *Trinity Royal* and *Holy Ghost*, the carrack *George* and the balingers *Nicholas*, *Gabriel Harfleur* and *Little John*. Others may well have taken part, as the masters of the sailing ships *Rodcogge*, *Grand Gabriel*, *Nicholas*, *Katherine* and *Thomas* were ordered to press sailors on 3 June. Nineteen royal shipmasters were granted annual salaries in August, and it's possible that, as well as being a measure designed to keep a good team together, this was also a reward for their recent service in battle. If this is correct, it would suggest that most of the royal fleet took part. It's also highly probable that the 1,000-ton great ship *Jesus* joined Huntingdon's force. Crewed by 200 men, the ship set sail from Winchelsea on its first voyage on 28 June, easily in time to join Huntingdon's expedition. It is improbable that a (literally) huge asset like the *Jesus* would have been left out, when the other two great ships were already sailing with reduced crews.[150]

The 1417 Battle and the Invasion

Huntingdon finally met the French and Genoese in battle on 25 July. One English source claims that the action was off La Hogue ('Hogges') on the eastern side of the Cherbourg Peninsula. The Italian chronicler Morosini merely states that it took place in the Channel between Southampton and Harfleur. However, in the pay account that he submitted for the Huntingdon expedition, Robert Shadde, master of the balinger *Nicholas*, says that the expedition went to *Seynhed*. A chart from 1646 shows that this was an alternative name for the Chef de Caux.

The French already knew that another English invasion was in the offing. The Genoese were anchored off Normandy with some 700 soldiers aboard, under the command of the Bastard of Bourbon. According to the St Denys chronicler, the English fleet had set sail about 29 June with a large number of big vessels, 2,000 men-at-arms and 1,500 'good archers'. The date and the presence of big ships is backed up by the English sources, though St Denys mistakenly believed that the fleet was commanded by the Duke of Clarence rather than the Earl of Huntingdon.

According to a Venetian report made just over three weeks after the battle, the fighting started at dawn and lasted barely three hours. The report had

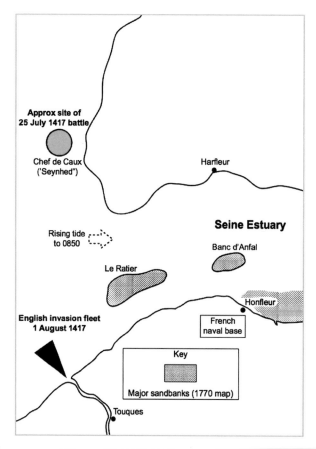

67 The likely general location of the 1417 battle off the Chef de Caux, and the site of the 1417 invasion.

first-hand, detailed information about the carracks that were captured (see below and Appendix 2), which suggests that its account of the battle is very credible. The action began with some ships ramming each other, smashing away forecastles, followed by grappling and boarding. St Denys speaks of a 'hail' of projectiles passing between the fleets, in which many more died on the English side. However, when it came to boarding, the English had the advantage – probably due in the main to the great ships. Details of the gear lost by the *Holy Ghost* in this battle show that the enemy got into the ship once again – they took various items away with them, including a gun – but the vessel does not seem to have suffered as badly as it did at Harfleur.

The well-informed Venetian report stated very accurately that four Genoese carracks were taken, and gave their sizes. It goes on to say that twenty-six ships of between 350 to 400 *botte* (175–200 tons) were also provided by the Castilians and the Basques. The military contingent in the fleet comprised about 800 Genoese men-at-arms, crossbowmen and lances, plus about 1,500–1,600 Spanish soldiers. There were many dead in the battle, including 140–150 Frenchmen who threw themselves overboard, presumably to escape death at the hands of English. It was a disaster for the French and Genoese. The latter withdrew their remaining ships to Brittany, not daring to go against the English again; the captured carracks, St Denys says, 'were sent gloriously to the king of England as trophies of their victory'.

Huntingdon returned in triumph to Southampton around 29 July with his four prize carracks, which were soon added to the royal fleet and rechristened *Andrew*, *Christopher*, *Paul* and *Peter*. Henry promised Huntingdon £1,000 as a reward for taking the carracks, though he was still owed it in 1423.[151] One piece of royal largesse that was dispensed was the grant of annual salaries to nineteen royal shipmasters on 12 August.[152]

Counting great ships and carracks, Henry V now had one of the most powerful war fleets in Europe, north or south. In military terms, the victories of 1416 and 1417 fully justified the huge sums spent on the great ships and the rest of the royal fleet. Those victories had broken the naval opposition fielded by the French and left the coast of Normandy undefended. On 1 August 1417, less than a week after the battle, Henry disembarked from the *Jesus* at the small port of Touques in Normandy. With him was a large invasion army.

After the Invasion

The 1417 invasion army numbered just over 10,800 soldiers, along with servants, craftsmen and others. We know that they were transported in at least 233 English and Dutch ships but the true figure was probably a good deal higher. Such was the urgency in making the fleet ready for Normandy, and keeping it in repair after the invasion, that between July and mid-October the master shipwright and probably the entire shipwright team building the *Grace Dieu* were diverted to fleet maintenance work.[153]

The invasion was followed by a land campaign that lasted several years. It was primarily a war of sieges: Caen fell to Henry on 4 September, Alençon in October, Falaise in February 1418 and Cherbourg the following September. By the autumn of 1418, the English controlled most of Normandy south

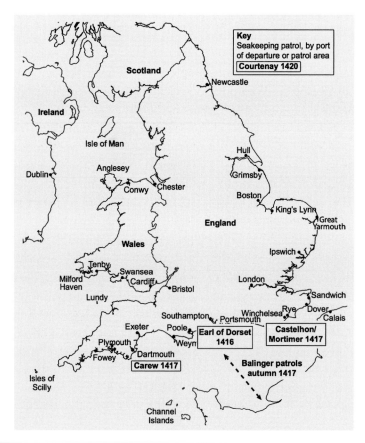

68 Sea patrols, 1416–17.

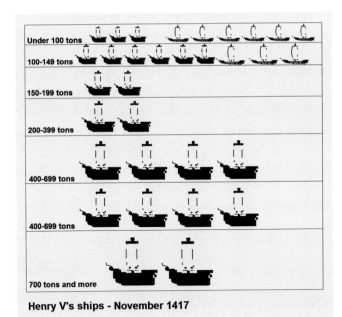

69 Operational vessels in the English royal fleet, November 1417.

Henry V's ships - November 1417

and west of the mouth of the Seine. The next challenge was to cross the great river, and that required the capture of the regional capital – Rouen.[154]

The scale of English naval activity was greatly reduced between the late summer of 1417 and the spring of 1418, but it did not cease entirely. The balinger *Nicholas* (probably along with other vessels) was used to defend the landing area at Touques until 27 September, to secure Henry's supply line from England. Two hundred and thirty-three English and Dutch transports were released from royal service in Normandy on 1 September, but this may have been premature. On 18 October, a public proclamation was made in England that anyone who wanted to take victuals to Caen could do so without paying customs duties, suggesting that not enough supplies were getting across the Channel.

On 30 September, the *Nicholas* and some other royal balingers set sail from Caen, patrolling the area between there and the Isle of Wight. The operation lasted until 22 December, when the *Nicholas* returned to Southampton. With 121 crew packed into the balinger's 120-ton hull, the autumn and winter weather is likely to have made it an exceptionally uncomfortable and miserable voyage. Once back in Southampton, the vessel stayed in harbour until the spring.[155]

The royal fleet reached its peak strength in the autumn of 1417, with thirty-two operational vessels (see plate 69), and the River Hamble came into full-time use as a fleet anchorage in November 1417. There was still a very real fear of a seaborne attack on the fleet and a company of forty-one archers was recruited to guard the royal ships in the Southampton area from 27 November to 27 February 1418. The same fear motivated the construction of a new tower at the mouth of Portsmouth Harbour, which began in January 1418. Its aim was to defend the harbour, the town and the surrounding area. Although much altered over the centuries, this fortification still survives, as the Round Tower (see plate 19c).[156]

8

FEAR AND VICTORY, 1418–22

Seakeeping and the Siege of Rouen

The year 1418 saw yet more seakeeping voyages, with the largest force led by Sir John Arundel. Arundel went to sea as the deputy of the Duke of Exeter, with 365 men-at-arms and 776 archers, as well as Lord Castelhon and Sir John Mortimer. The fleet was to include two great ships, three carracks, four barges and six balingers – fifteen vessels in all – in service for six months, though in fact the fleet was apparently only at sea from 20 April to 13 July. The patrol was mustered at Southampton in March.

However, the overall composition of the force was very different from, say, the seakeeping patrol of 1415, which was predominantly a force of medium-sized sailing ships. The 1418 patrol consisted mostly of big sailing ships and oared vessels. A similar pattern can be seen in the 1420 seakeeping fleet and in the changing composition of the royal fleet itself. It seems that English ideas about naval warfare were changing, and changing quite rapidly. The small and medium-sized sailing ships of the kind that Henry acquired in the early years of his reign, began to disappear from the ranks of the king's ships between 1418 and 1420, and most were not replaced. It does look as if they were no longer considered fit to stand in the medieval equivalent of the 'line of battle', fighting carracks and other great vessels (Appendix 2).[157]

The French and Genoese were not the only seaborne enemies to concern the English. Attacks by Scottish vessels in the North Sea were also becoming a problem, and in late April 1418 a commission was issued for the arrest of four 'great ships' and four balingers on the east coast 'for safekeeping the sea against the king's enemies of Scotland'. The force was to muster at Hull and carry 120 men-at-arms and 240 archers. In the end, eight vessels were scraped together for the operation, but they were all balingers and barges, with no 'great ships'.[158]

70 Sea patrols 1418.

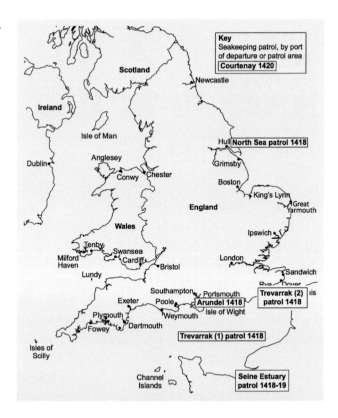

Arundel's expedition returned to Southampton in July. In that same month, William Soper became 'surveyor of the king's ships, carracks and balingers', acting effectively as a second clerk of the king's ships. The great ship *Grace Dieu* was blessed by the Bishop of Bangor in July, although the vessel was not ready for sea until the spring of 1420.[159]

In early July 1418, there were renewed warnings of an attack on the king's ships at Southampton. The people of Hampshire were told to organise coast watches, and Soper was given powers to conscript locals to garrison the ships, if necessary. The same fear of surprise attack clearly lay behind a new naval operation. Eight balingers and barges, six of them royal, were sent out to patrol the southern and western parts of the English Channel between 25 July and 29 September. They carried fifty-eight men-at-arms and 128 archers, led by a soldier named Thomas Trevarrak, though the patrol was only strong enough to act as an 'early warning' group. Its dispatch was doubtless connected with plans for the siege of Rouen, which began a few days after the force left port. The aim of the patrol was probably to provide extra security in the Channel while a large part of the English army's attention was focused on the city.[160]

The English besieged Rouen for over four months, from 30 July or 1 August to the middle of January 1419. Rouen was heavily fortified, the site of the Clos des Galées, and commanded the routes north and west of the Seine. It was also the capital of Normandy, a position of great political and psychological significance. The French were determined to hold the city, and the English were just as determined to take it.

The French themselves destroyed the Clos des Galées, which in any case had proved to be a useless asset. The English secured control of the Seine downstream of Rouen, making it easy to bring supplies up the river from England and Harfleur to Henry's siege lines. Rouen lay on the north bank of the Seine, and the English encircled the landward sides of the city. French attempts at blockade-running from the sea were stopped by English vessels in the river, and the English also used a large chain to close the Seine near Rouen. The French had still managed to hold the Seine bridge, but in order to get around it, and cut off the city from inland resupply, Henry had some of his vessels dragged overland round the bridge and then launched into the Seine upstream of Rouen.

Three small Portuguese galleys were used to help defend the Seine Estuary during the siege. Royal ships involved in the siege itself included the *Margaret* and at least two balingers, the 120-ton *Nicholas* and the 20-ton *Swan*. It's possible that the lightly built *Swan* was one of the vessels dragged overland at Rouen. The resupply of the army from England carried on over the autumn

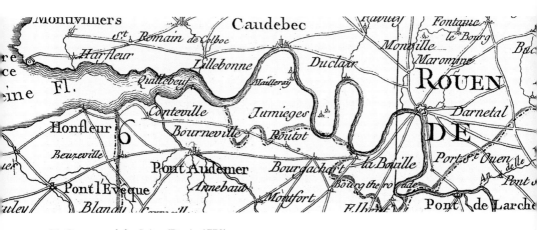

71 Rouen and the Seine (Denis, 1770).

and winter, and included the use of some royal balingers to rush priority cargoes of gunpowder, saltpetre and sulphur to Caen. Henry was using waterborne resupply, as well as the tactics of seakeeping and blockade, to support his land campaign.

Rouen's sizeable population was already swollen by large numbers of refugees from the countryside, and as the autumn went on, their food began to run out. A large number of poor, sick and old people were driven out, to save supplies, on the apparent assumption that the English would feed them and let them go. This overestimated Henry's capacity for mercy. Many of the refugees died, trapped between the siege lines and the city. In the end, as French relief attempts failed, Rouen surrendered.[161]

Another small-scale seakeeping operation was organised for early November 1418. Some balingers and *passagers* were sent out from Dover with sixty men-at-arms and 120 archers, again under Trevarrak's leadership. The patrol lasted until Christmas and was probably designed to reinforce English control of the Seine Estuary.[162]

The Hamble Anchorage and Coastal Defence

The River Hamble lies on the eastern side of Southampton Water, a few miles below Southampton itself, and in 1417 it became the main anchorage for the English royal fleet. There was a pressing need for a secure base on the south coast due to the course of the naval war, the shift of most of the royal ships from the Thames to Southampton and the Franco-Genoese attacks of 1416.

The Hamble became well known in the seventeenth and eighteenth centuries as a place for building warships, and the factors that made this possible were probably similar to those that made it attractive as a fleet base for Henry V's ships. The Hamble offered shelter from the prevailing westerly winds: in 1698, a Navy Board report described the river as 'narrow, but deep and safe'; it was also a location where later Georgian builders found they could launch big warship hulls.

Good shelter and water depth would have been key considerations for Henry's officials. The loss of the valuable carrack *Agase* in an open anchorage at Southampton was a warning of what could happen in a storm. The Hamble's comparatively narrow mouth also made it easier to defend from the sea, a very important consideration, given how close the French and Genoese raiders got to the English fleet in 1416. The river was also home to

72 The River Hamble as shown on the first edition of the Ordnance Survey Map, 1810.

three small ports, Hamble-le-Rice (modern Hamble), Hook, on the opposite bank of the river and Bursledon upstream.

Work had started on a tower at Portsmouth in January 1418 to guard the harbour entrance (see plate 19c), and the Hamble acquired its own fort just over a year later. It cost at least £125 to construct, was built of wood and called the 'Bulwark'. The work was supervised by William Soper, and the fort was probably complete by late spring or early summer 1419.

From January 1419 there were fresh rumours that enemy carracks were likely to appear off the Isle of Wight. By 3 March, Henry had received frightening intelligence that a large Castilian fleet was at sea, planning to attack England, 'and especially to burn and destroy the ships and navy of the realm, most of all the ships which are at Southampton and Portsmouth'. Coastal counties from Cornwall to Norfolk were alerted, and additional defence works were put in hand at Hamble. Two great iron chains, each 80 fathoms long (480ft/146m), were made for 'chaining up outside the port

73 Schematic
illustration of the
nature of the Hamble
defences *c.* 1420:
the location of the
Bulwark is uncertain,
though it would
have been easier
to reinforce from
inland if it was on
the left-hand side of
the river.

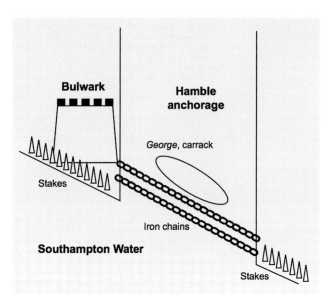

74 A coastal warning beacon depicted on a fifteenth-century mural in the church of
St Peter, Shorwell, Isle of Wight.

of Hamble', and carpenters and labourers were put to work 'night and day' driving wooden piles and stakes into the shoreline. The stakes were probably sharpened timbers, like those used to impale cavalry horses in land battles; here they were for use against landing boats.

The Bulwark was garrisoned by a group of soldiers from 1 August 1420 to 23 July 1421, with the experienced soldier Thomas Trevarrak as captain. The troops worked alongside two watchmen to keep guard and maintain surveillance 'night and day' against a surprise attack. The soldiers were also stationed in the carrack *George*, which was moored by the harbour chains and acted as a guard ship. No attack ever came, but the defence preparations were serious and careful. The Bulwark survived into the 1420s, but its eventual fate is not known.[163]

1419–20: The Spanish Threat

By 1419, the land war in France was very much going Henry V's way, with more and more of the Normandy coastline falling under English control. For all that, there were fears of a naval threat from another ally of the French, Castile.

The report that a force of carracks was heading for the Isle of Wight led to the despatch of a strong seakeeping patrol. Commanded by the Earl of Salisbury, it included three Venetian carracks and was at sea from 18 January to 13 February. No attack materialised, but the apprehension remained, and led to the raid warnings issued in March. That same month, the Earl of Huntingdon was ordered to guard the Seine Estuary.

Another seakeeping patrol out in the English Channel from 1 March to 1 August, led by Hugh Courtenay (son of the Earl of Devon) and Sir Thomas Carew, with 380 men-at-arms and 780 archers. The fleet consisted of royal vessels – three carracks, five ships and eight balingers, with 1,178 sailors in all. Unlike some other patrols, it had very specific objectives. It was to patrol the Normandy coast between Dieppe and Cherbourg, and defend the mouth of the Seine. Perhaps bearing in mind the futile chase of the Genoese carrack by the Calais balingers in 1416, Courtenay was told that if part of the fleet went off in pursuit of enemy vessels, then some ships had to be left to guard the Seine. The expedition did not fight any major battles, but it did capture a 290-ton Spanish sailing ship, later acquired by the king and rechristened as the *Holy Ghost Spain*.

75 Sea patrols 1419–21.

The English fear of Spain was not just paranoia. Spanish vessels had served the French in 1416 and 1417, and France and Castile had concluded an alliance in June 1419. Under the Treaty of Segovia, the Spanish agreed to supply the French with forty large ships, twenty galleys and 4,200 sailors and soldiers. Shortly after, a copy of the treaty fell into Bayonnese hands, when one of their balingers seized a Spanish ship that was carrying a royal official. Bayonne, in southern Gascony and close to the Spanish border, was one of the most consistently loyal of medieval England's overseas possessions. Capturing the document was a real intelligence coup, but its contents made disturbing reading. The information was forwarded to Henry as soon as possible, on 22 July.

The Franco-Spanish plan was for forty armed Spanish ships to go to Belle Isle (off the west coast of southern Brittany) to take on a French admiral,

Braquemont, and soldiers sent by the Dauphin (the future Charles VII), who was now the focus of French opposition to the English. The fleet would then sail to Scotland, another French ally, and ferry Scottish troops to France to fight on the Dauphin's side. The Bayonnese also expected the Spanish to lay siege to Bayonne, and feared their defences were inadequate. Unlike some of the vague rumours that masqueraded as intelligence, both the Spanish fleet and the threat to Bayonne were real.

The 22 July letter reached England quickly and led to rapid action, at least by medieval standards. The safest route for the Spanish was up the west coast of England and Wales, and on 12 August the government ordered the sheriff of Devon to arrest eight ships and balingers and send them out to intercept the enemy ships. It was soon realised that eight vessels would not have much chance of stopping forty, and on 24 August additional orders for ships went to Somerset, Dorset and Hampshire.

Intercepting a fleet on the high seas was always a chancy proposition in the days before aerial reconnaissance and radar. The Spanish fleet, accompanied by some French ships, reached Scotland without even being sighted by the English. They embarked 6,000 Scottish troops in September, and carried them safely to France, arriving in October 1419. The failure to catch the Spanish was followed in late December by a battle off La Rochelle, in which a fleet of Spanish and French ships destroyed an English and Hanseatic merchant convoy, with heavy loss of life.

Aside from tying up English resources in sea patrols and coastal defence, the main outcome of the Spanish intervention was to take the Scottish troops to France. These men bolstered the French war effort, and in 1421 some of them took part in a battle at Baugé in which Henry's brother, the Duke of Clarence, was killed and the English were defeated.

The sea battle off La Rochelle was a worrying defeat for the English, but it was nowhere near as serious as the apocalyptic raid or fleet-to-fleet encounter they had feared. With their great ships and carracks, the English might have been victorious in a sea battle with the Spanish. However, given the signs of manpower problems in the royal fleet, and the decline of the English carrack force, the outcome might not have been so certain. In the end, as Nicholas Rodger writes, it was Spanish internal politics that settled the matter, with a coup in July 1420. The new regime withdrew Spanish support for France and ended the naval threat to England.[164]

The Royal Sailing Vessels, 1418–22

The start of 1418 saw the last major disaster suffered by Henry's ships out at sea: the *Little Marie* sank somewhere between Guérande and Cornwall on 5 January. Over the next three years, seven other small and medium-sized sailing ships disappeared from the royal fleet, if less dramatically. They were sold off or given away in poor condition, or in some cases docked for repairs that were never made (see Appendix 2). By 1422, the only two survivors of the 1413–15 fleet that were still in royal hands, and would sail again, were the ships *Thomas* and *Grand Marie*. Although a few more sailing vessels of less than 300 tons had come into the king's fleet between 1417 and 1420 as prizes, there was no concerted effort to replace the lost small- to medium-sized sailing ships.

Parallel with this, the carrack fleet was deteriorating, because the Crown was unable to maintain most of the captured vessels. Significantly, no carracks were available for the last big seakeeping expedition of Henry's reign. The *Andrew* and the *Marie Hampton* sank at anchor in the Hamble in 1420. The *Paul* had to be beached in the same year, and in 1421 the *Peter* was laid up in a dock at Southampton. The *Marie Sandwich* stayed afloat, but by 1422 the *George* and *Christopher* were the only two carracks left in usable condition.

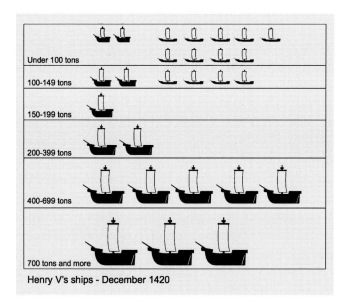

Henry V's ships - December 1420

76 Operational vessels in the English royal fleet, December 1420.

With the gradual disappearance of the smaller sailing ships and the decay of the carracks, the royal fleet became a force that mainly relied on the great ships and oared fighting vessels.[165]

Mutiny in the Solent, 1420

Something very odd happened when the last big sea patrol of Henry's reign gathered in the Solent in the spring of 1420: there was a mutiny. Even stranger, the mutineers included both ordinary crew and the fleet commander, Hugh Courtenay, now Earl of Devon (1389–1422). The document detailing the events was discovered and published by Susan Rose in the 1970s.[166]

In part, the mutiny had something to do with a mass refusal to be mustered, that is, for men to have their names entered in the records of the voyage. Mustering was essential, to combat fraud by checking that pay was going to men who really existed, and that an expedition had its agreed complement of sailors and soldiers. This fleet was due to take around 500 men-at-arms and 1,000 archers to sea.

The force was divided into subsections led by William, Lord Botreaux (1389–1462), Sir Thomas Carew (1368?–1431) and John Hawley the Younger of Dartmouth (c. 1384–1436). Botreaux was a Somerset landowner and Agincourt veteran, and Carew's lands were in Devon. Carew and Botreaux 'humbly' obeyed the royal command to muster their men. These particular Westcountrymen did as they were told, but there was trouble with other men of the west in the fleet, not least the Earl of Devon, who for some reason refused point-blank to have his men mustered. The Devon-based John William was also present, as master of the great ship *Jesus*, and did likewise. Hawley's vessel could not be reached by the commissioners, due to a storm.

Things got worse when the muster commissioners boarded the great ship *Grace Dieu*. One of the ship's quartermasters, a Dartmouth man named William Duke, violently snatched the muster roll from the ship's clerk and threatened to chuck it into the sea. Once the ships had set sail from Southampton, nine men (including some from Dartmouth, Plymouth and Tavistock), 'with many others' rose up against the Earl of Devon, the master and the rest of the crew. They forced them to sail to St Helen's on the Isle of Wight, and then refused to go back to sea. A servant of one of the commissioners made the mistake of asking one of the mutineers why he didn't want to be mustered, and got roughed up for his pains.

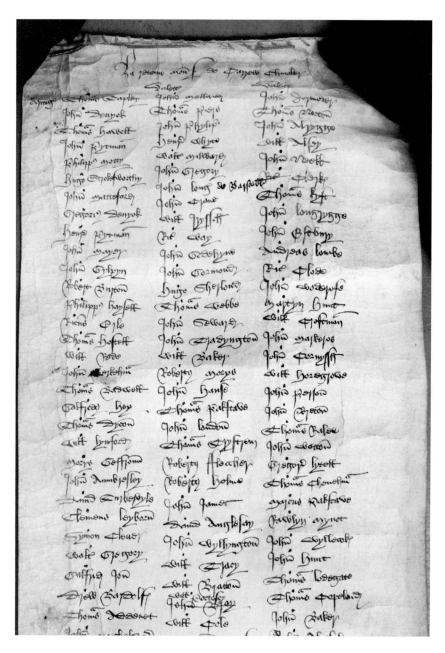

77 Part of the muster of the military retinue of Sir Thomas Carew aboard the great ship *Holy Ghost* at Southampton, 14 May 1420. A muster made 'humbly', unlike some. (TNA E101/49/35, m 7, The National Archives, Kew)

Rose suggests that the prohibition of shore leave during the expedition, coupled with overcrowding and bad food, may have helped to whip up tension in the ships. There may also have been some trepidation about sailing in the *Grace Dieu*, the biggest ship any of those present had ever seen. These reasons may certainly have contributed to the development of a mutinous atmosphere, but the first three factors were common to all naval expeditions of the period. Also, it does not explain why the mutiny included the fleet commander, who enjoyed better conditions than anyone else, and was carrying out his task under contract to the king. Perhaps the earl was reacting to a perceived personal slight of some kind, though in the end he apparently allowed the musters (below). Mutinous feelings seem to have been particularly strong among some of the ordinary Devon men in the fleet. Perhaps it was in part a revolt by pressed men, torn from home – certainly two of the ringleaders were not seamen by profession, for one was a tailor and the other a forest worker.

Surprisingly, in view of what happened, we do know what the composition and planned crew sizes of the fleet were supposed to be:

Ship and type	Master	Constable	Carpenter	Mariners	Boys
Grace Dieu GS	William Payn	1	1	191	6
Jesus GS	John William	1	1	131	6
Holy Ghost GS	Jordan Brownyng	1	1	93	4
Trinity Royal GS	William Yalton	1	1	93	4
Grand Marie S	Richard Walssh	–	–	37	2
Nicholas BL	Robert Shadde	–	–	95	4
George II BL	Edward Hopier	–	–	96	3
Valentine BL	Richard Rowe	–	–	77	2
Falcon BL	William Cheke	–	–	67	2
Swan BL	Robert Dolyng	–	–	37	
James BL	William Proute	–	–	37	2
Gabriel Harfleur BL	Andrew Godfray	–	–	37	2
Mary of Dartmouth S (200 tons)	Henry Hamond	–	–	41	3

In total, there were 1,032 mariners and just forty-two boys. As less than 4 per cent of the ships' crews were boys, a very much lower proportion than in the 1413–16 period, this may sound like an argument against a shortage of sailors in England. The balingers were relatively well manned: they had to be, or they could not move under oars. However, closer examination shows that the great ships, and probably the *Grand Marie*, were seriously undercrewed. The complement of the *Grace Dieu*, 199 men and boys, sounds enormous, but it was no more than the *Jesus* had first carried in 1417, and the *Jesus* was 400 tons smaller than the *Grace Dieu*. Each of the first three great ships had carried around 200 sailors in the years between 1415 and 1417, suggesting that this was the norm for these vessels. On this basis, in 1420 the *Jesus* had just under 70 per cent of its proper complement, and the *Holy Ghost* and *Trinity Royal* had about half theirs. If the great ships, the *Grace Dieu* included, had insufficient crews, they may have sailed badly, terrifying those on board and contributing to the mutinous atmosphere.[167]

There is an odd footnote to this incident. A well-known letter of the period, reliably attributed to Humphrey, Duke of Gloucester, speaks of the Earl of Devonshire actually making his muster for this voyage. The letter was addressed to Henry V and the relevant passage goes as follows (spelling modernised):

> Your great ship the *Grace Dieu* is ever as ready and is the fairest that man saw
> I trow in good faith [meaning 'I truly believe'] … and this day the Earl of
> Devonshire my cousin made his muster in her and all the others have their
> muster the same time that shall go to the sea.

Curiously, the muster rolls of the Earl of Devonshire and Lord Botreaux do survive for this voyage, but at the time of writing they are listed as 'missing' by The National Archives. If located, they might help to clear up some of the mystery behind the Solent revolt, but whatever caused it, the mutiny ensured that medieval England's greatest warship got no further than the Isle of Wight.[168]

The Last Years of Henry's Navy

In September 1419, John the Fearless, Duke of Burgundy, was assassinated by a servant of the French Dauphin during a meeting to discuss an alliance. Whether the murder was planned or not, the Dauphin was disgraced, and this single, violent death removed two strong candidates from the line of succession to the deranged French king, Charles VI. It also made Henry V much more credible as a potential successor. The fractured French political situation and Henry's military successes eventually led to the Treaty of Troyes in 1420, which recognised Henry as Charles VI's heir, and gave him the hand of Princess Katherine of France in marriage.

This did not stop the war though, as the forces of French opposition coalesced around the Dauphin. Signs of war-weariness were starting to appear in England, along with renewed fears of old enemies. The 1420 and 1421 Parliaments also called for action against the Scots, who were making renewed attacks on the border and at sea. Henry was also starting to experience greater problems in funding the French conflict. There was even a fear, expressed in Parliament, that if England did become part of an Anglo-French dual monarchy, the French side would dominate. England may have won a great triumph in France, but in the early 1420s the country seems to have been less than easy with the consequences of victory.[169]

The activity of the English fleet wound down in 1421-22. The last seakeeping voyage of Henry's reign was led by Sir William Bardolf in the spring of 1421. It left from Dover, and was a mixed force with four royal balingers and six balingers and barges from the Cinque Ports. The Spanish threat ceased to be a factor, and the naval defeat of France was made complete by English occupation of most of the coastline of northern France, with a few exceptions, such as Le Crotey. Given that no royal vessels had been taken by the enemy in the great battles or seakeeping patrols, there is some irony in the fact that in August 1421 vessels from Le Crotey were able to capture a small royal ship, the *Marie Breton*.[170]

Perhaps because there was now less of a naval threat, some of the masters of the royal balingers engaged in piracy. Six of them seem to have resorted to acts of sea robbery in 1421. Four of these men underwent temporary arrest, though they never seem to have suffered anything worse.[171]

On 10 June 1421, the royal balinger *Nicholas* transported Henry V from Sandwich to Calais. The king was returning to France with an army of reinforcements, but it was the last time he would ever see England. As far as anyone knows, it was also the last time in his life that he set foot on any of the ships in his navy.[172]

Henry died on 31 August 1422, of a disease probably caught in a siege camp. The final act of Henry's navy that directly involved the king came in October. A fleet of ships was arrested in ports from Great Yarmouth to Sussex, and around the end of that month they carried Henry's embalmed body and his funeral party from Calais to Dover.[173]

9

AFTER HENRY

The Decline of the Royal Fleet

William Soper became a travelling salesman after Henry died, riding across the south and west of England. His purpose was to sell off the royal ships, which he did very effectively. Between 1422 and 1425, nineteen of the king's ships went to private owners, raising £1,000.

The ostensible reason for the royal council's order to sell was to raise money to pay off the late king's debts. However, the money brought in by selling the ships was one and a half times more than was required, so something else was going on here. As Susan Rose suggests, the underlying reasons for the sale were both strategic and financial. With Normandy conquered and Spain no longer an enemy, the naval war was over. There was nothing much for the king's ships to do, certainly not enough to justify the maintenance of a large and expensive fleet. The annual salary payments to royal shipmasters also stopped, breaking up Henry's team of seafarers, though many of these men had already voted with their feet and left to pursue other work.

By the mid-1420s, only the four great ships and two balingers were left in government hands. This is not to say that the idea of having a royal fleet was immediately abandoned. The money and care lavished on the great ships in the 1420s and early 1430s does not suggest that anyone was thinking of getting rid of these powerful vessels, and even the Bulwark was kept in repair for a time. The ships could have formed the nucleus of a new fleet, if needed. One of the lessons of Henry's time was surely that it did not take very long to create a navy almost from scratch. There may also have been a reluctance to dispose of vessels so intimately linked with the personality, achievements, prestige and memory of the most successful English king since Edward III. [174]

Most of the money spent on the great ships in the 1420s was devoted to keeping them afloat. Shipkeepers, shipwrights and caulkers were employed,

78 The sales of royal ships, 1421–25.

Scotland

Newcastle

Ireland

Isle of Man

Hull

Anglesey

Grimsby

Dublin

Conwy Chester

Boston

King's Lynn

England

Great Yarmouth

London Thames:
6 ships
2 balingers
1 galley

Ipswich

Wales

London

Tenby

Swansea

Milford Haven

Cardiff

Bristol

1 carrack

Lundy

Sandwich

Southampton

Winchelsea

Rye

Dover

Portsmouth

Calais

Exeter

Poole

Plymouth

Isle of Wight

Chichester:
1 ship

Weymouth

4 carracks
3 ships
1 balinger
1 barge

Dartmouth

Fowey

3 balingers
1 barge

Isles of Scilly

1 balinger

Saltash:
1 balinger

Channel Islands

and large quantities of caulking materials were purchased, along with sixteen new pumps and pump spares. The *Holy Ghost* proved to be the leakiest vessel. In 1423, a Welsh *dyver* named Davy Owen was employed to dive underneath the ship to block up cracks in the hull that were inaccessible from inside. This is perhaps the earliest record of a diver employed in such a role, but Davy's hard and dangerous work was of little avail, for the leaks continued. Finally, the mast and rigging were removed in spring 1426 and the great vessel was docked at Bursledon on 21 June that year. The initial intention was to repair the ship: heavy stocks were laid to take the keel and 100 shores or props were bought to keep the hull upright, but after several years, the *Holy Ghost* was abandoned.

The *Trinity Royal* was the next vessel to be docked. It was towed from its moorings at Bursledon in 1429 or 1430, stripped of its mast and laid up in a large *fossura* or 'digging' in the mud at Hamble. Nothing was said in the accounts about trying to repair the ship, so this hole was probably intended

151

as the ship's grave. Plans for the *Jesus* were less final when it was its turn to be docked in late 1432 or 1433. The avowed purpose was to rebuild the ship, but nothing happened and the derelict was finally sold off in 1446.

The last of the great ships, the *Grace Dieu*, never realised its warlike potential, but it could and did serve as a symbol of English power. In January 1430, a fleet of Florentine trading galleys paid a call on Southampton. It was commanded by Luca di Maso degli Albizzi, who was entertained by various Southampton notables, including William Soper. Soper took him to the Hamble to dine on the *Grace Dieu*. This well-travelled man was mightily impressed by the ship, so much so that he had it measured. The units he used can be interpreted in different ways, but they point to a vessel over 164ft (50m) in length and 49ft (15m) wide, with a forestage that stood around 50ft (15.2m) above the water. He also said that the mainmast was something over 190ft (57.9m) in height.[175]

The upper part of the *Grace Dieu*'s mainmast was taken down in 1432, along with its great masthead pulley and topcastle. Two years later, in the summer of 1434, the ship was stripped of much of its remaining gear and cleaned of ballast and mud. On 1 August, the *Grace Dieu* was floated into a dock made in the mud at Bursledon. It wasn't as elaborate as the docks for the *Holy Ghost* and *Jesus*, but attempts were made to deflect the current from the hull and the site was enclosed with a protective hedge.

At some point between 1427 and 1433 an unusual structure was built at Southampton. It was called a 'hovel store', had a thatched roof and was 140ft long by 14ft wide (42.7 x 4.3m). The building was used to store masts and spars that would not fit in the storehouse rented in the town for the king's ships. By this time, a lot of the gear stored at Southampton and in the Tower of London was deteriorating badly. The three sails and three bonnets from the *Grace Dieu* were sold in January 1435 for the not inconsiderable sum of £30, despite the fact that they had been eaten and holed by 'rats, mice and great worms'. Some of the purchasers of old sails were painters, such as John Stafford of Southampton, who bought another vermin-eaten sail in April 1436. It would be interesting to know what he painted on this recycled canvas.

On the night of 7 January 1439, the *Grace Dieu* was struck by lightning during a winter storm and caught fire. The pitch and tar in the hull will have helped the flames to spread quickly, and by morning the great ship was a pile of charred debris. Soper immediately started a salvage effort to recover usable ironwork from the ship's remains, and in January and February close on eight tonnes (7,840kg) of clenchnails, roves, bolts, spikes, chains and other metalwork were pulled out of the Hamble mud.

The salvage of materials from the great ships carried on through the 1430s and into the early 1440s, with cabin boards, iron chains, leadwork, nails and other things taken to the store at Southampton. The rotting and rusted items in the store were still being systematically listed – Soper even kept the burnt stump of the *Grace Dieu*'s mainmast.[176]

On 7 April 1442, William Soper retired as keeper of the king's ships and handed over what was mostly a collection of junk to Richard Clyvedon, another royal servant. Clyvedon was in office until 1452, with no budget save what could be earned by selling things. The old Hamble harbour chains were broken up and melted down, and there was a final phase of salvage in the Hamble. Two huge anchors, one from the *Grace Dieu* and one from the *Holy Ghost*, were measured prior to being loaned to a ship going in an expedition to relieve the embattled English enclave in Gascony, but events overtook the expedition. Gascony fell to the French, and the anchors were never sent. And with that, the administrative afterlife of Henry V's navy came to an end.[177]

But Henry's navy was not forgotten, at least for a generation or two. *The Libel of English Policy*, a political poem about sea power written by an unknown author in 1436 and 1437, drew lessons from Henry V's reign. The writer saw a particular need for England to have a strong navy and to control the surrounding sea, particularly the 'Narrow Sea' that divided the country from the Continent. The poem also dripped with nostalgia for the glories of Henry's day, at a time when things were starting to go very badly for the English in France. Famously, it used the image on an English noble, a gold coin, as a symbol for the sea power the author believed the country should wield (spelling and punctuation modernised):

For 4 things our noble showeth to me,
King, ship and sword, and power of the sea …
Henry the Fifth, what was his purposing,
When at (South) Hampton he made the great dromons,
Which passed other great ships of all the commons
The Trinity, the Grace Dieu, the Holy Ghost,
And other more which as now be lost,
What hope ye was the king's great intent
Of the ships, and in what mind he meant?
It was not else that he cast to be
Lord round about, environ of the sea.

79 A gold noble of
Edward III. This imagery,
with its questionable claim
to sovereignty over the sea,
was repeated in one form or
another on English coins until
the reign of Henry VIII. It also
gave inspiration to the writer
of the *Libel of English Policy*.
(Nicolas, 1847, p.223)

Twenty years later, Henry's sea war was still alive as oral history. An account of a disastrous battle between English and Spanish ships in 1458, ends with the remark that 'as men have said, there was not so great a battle on the sea this forty winter.'[178]

Thereafter, the naval history of Henry V's reign became something that only scholars recalled. Shakespeare's *Henry V* briefly described the fleet mustered for the 1415 invasion, but neither the sea battles nor the 1417 invasion suited his dramatic purposes, and they don't get a mention.

The Rediscovery of the *Grace Dieu*

Something unusual was reported in an 1859 guidebook entry about Bursledon:

> In a creek about a mile above the village, some timbers are still to be seen at very low water. This is supposed to have been one of the four Danish ships said to have been burned here by the Saxons about 877 … Many pieces of timber are preserved by the inhabitants.

This 'Viking' wreck was the subject of some investigations, most notoriously by local landowner Francis Crawshay, who used gunpowder as an excavation aid. Some useful information was recovered, but the combined effects of Crawshay's explosive 'archaeology', souvenir hunting and deliberate demolition must have removed large parts of an already damaged and decayed ancient structure.

In the early 1930s, the wreck was examined by the eminent maritime historian R.C. Anderson. He realised that this huge, clinker-built hull must be medieval, because no big ships were built in England by this method

80 Drawing made from an 1870s photograph of work on the *Grace Dieu*. (Bowker, 1902)

81 The *Grace Dieu* on a falling tide, early 1980s.

after the late 1400s. He also knew about Henry V's fleet, and soon made the connection between the wreck and the documentary evidence for the *Grace Dieu*. Subsequent research has confirmed his identification.

There have been a number of studies of the vessel since the 1930s, and in 2005 it was surveyed using an acoustic sub-bottom profiler. This was able to create an accurate 3D image of the wreck using sound waves, revealing the

82 A glimpse of the remains of the great ship, 2015.

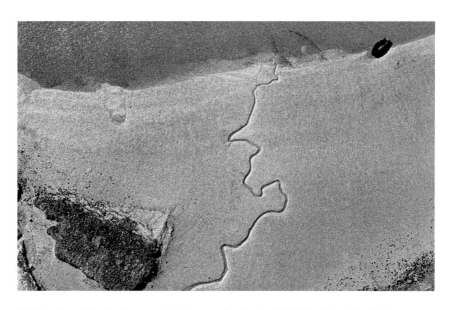

83 The *Grace Dieu* site, in an aerial photograph taken in 1979. The *Grace Dieu* lies just to the left of the derelict modern boat on the right of the photo. A large, vaguely ship-like impression is visible at the tideline on the left-hand side of the image – could this be the remains of Henry V's great ship *Holy Ghost*? (Historic England)

shape and depth of the hull in much greater detail than ever before. It showed that the remains of the ship measure at least 32.5m (106.5ft) in length, with a maximum width of 12.2m (40ft) and a depth of 2m (6.5ft). Given that the hull was of course longer and wider than its bottom, this gives credibility to the measurements taken by Albizzi in 1430.[179]

The *Grace Dieu* site was designated a Protected Wreck in 1974 under the 1973 Protection of Wrecks Act, which safeguards an area of 75m around the site from unauthorised disturbance. You cannot land within this zone without a special licence, but you can usually catch sight of some wreck timbers at very low tides from the opposite side of the river.[180]

The *Grace Dieu* is perhaps not the only trace of Henry's navy left in the Hamble. The remains of the *Holy Ghost* may lie downstream from the *Grace Dieu* (see plate 83). There is also the exciting possibility that the glutinous river mud might conceal the sunken carracks *Andrew* and *Marie Hampton*, portions of the medieval harbour defences and even the great ship *Trinity Royal*.

One way or another, the story of Henry V's navy is not yet over.

APPENDIX 1[181]

Henry V's Shipmasters: Summaries of Careers in Royal Service

Names in **bold** are those known to have been paid as retainers; ship types and tonnages in brackets

Master	Period in royal service	Sailing ships	Oared vessels	Crew sizes	No. of known voyages	Known voyages
John Arnold	1415 (part)		*Gabriel* (BL, 30t)	nk	1	English Channel
William atte Hethe	1417–*c.* 1420	*Marie Hampton* (CA, 500)		89	1	**English Channel**
John Bedell (Philip Webbe was also master in this period, exact dates nk)	*c.* 1420–22		*Marie Breton* (BG, tonnage nk)	nk	2+ possibly	English Channel
John Bolle/Bull	1416–20		*Little John* (BL, tonnage nk); *James* (BL, tonnage nk); *Falcon* (BL, 80t)	36	2+	**English Channel**
Thomas Brown	Between 1417 and 1420 (dates uncertain)		*Katherine Breton* (BL, tonnage nk)	nk	nk	English Channel
Jordan Brownyng	1415–*c.* 1422; 1425–27 (shipkeeper)	*Holy Ghost* (GS, 740/760t)		200	4+	**English Channel**

158

Master	Period in royal service	Sailing ships	Oared vessels	Crew sizes	No. of known voyages	Known voyages
William Cheke	**1417–22**	***Grand Marie* (S, 116/140t); *Paul* (CA, 600t); *Thomas* (S, 160t)**	***Falcon* (BL, 80t)**	**38–69**	**3**	**English Channel, Gascony**
John Cossard	1416		*James* (BL, tonnage nk)	nk	1	English Channel
Nicholas Dalton	c. 1417–18	*Thomas* (S, 160t)		nk	1	English Channel
William Delamare	1415–17	*Marie Breton* (S, 50t)		11	3+	Gascony, Irish Sea
John Dene	***c.* 1417–18**		***Katherine Breton* (BL, tonnage nk)**	**nk, but probably 10**	**1+?**	**English Channel**
Thomas Dene	1416–17		*Gabriel* (BL, 30t)	nk, but probably 42	2	English Channel
William Downynge/ Dowlynge (probably the same man)	c. 1419–20		*James* (BL, tonnage nk); *Swan* (BL, 20t)	nk, but probably 26	nk	English Channel?
Robert Dolynge/ Downynge	1420–21		*Swan* (BL, 20t)	26	2+	English Channel
William Elyot	1413–c. 1415		*Peter* (BL, 24t)	23	2	North Sea, English Channel
John Emete	1413–14	*Cog John* (S, 220t)		43	1	Gascony, Irish Sea
John/James Gerard	**1417**	***Peter* (CA, 600t)**		**100**	**nk**	**nk**
Andrew Godfray	***c.* 1417–22**		***Gabriel Harfleur* (BL, 40t)**	**44**	**2+**	**English Channel**
John Goffard	c. 1417		*James* (BL, tonnage nk)	nk	nk	nk
John Gronde	c. 1416–20	*Margaret* (S, 70t)		16	2+	Gascony, Irish Sea
Roger Hemmyng	c. 1417–18	*Marie Breton* (S, 50t)		nk	1+	Portugal (hired voyage)
Thomas Heyward	c. 1416–17		*George* II (BL, 120t)	143	2	English Channel

Master	Period in royal service	Sailing ships	Oared vessels	Crew sizes	No. of known voyages	Known voyages
Edward Hopier	1417–c. 1422		George II (BL, 120t)	nk, but probably approx. 140	2	English Channel
William Hore	1415–c. 1417 (possibly died 1417)	Thomas (S, 160t)		34	3	Gascony, English Channel
Ralph Huskard	1416–22	Grand Marie (S, 116/140t)	Anne (BL, 120t)	nk, but possibly 100	4+	English Channel, Gascony
John Jon	1417–23	Andrew (CA, 400t – shipkeeping only); Holy Ghost Spain (S, 290t)		nk	2	Gascony, North Sea
John Kyngeston	1413–18	Little Trinity (S, 120t, 1413–15); Katherine (S, 210t, 1415–18)		27–49	6	Gascony, North Sea, English Channel
Thomas Martyn	1417–18	Rodcogge (S, 120t)		25	1+	Gascony
John Merssh	1415–22	Katherine (S, 210t); George (CA, 600t, shipkeeping only); Andrew (CA, 400t); Marie Sandwich (CA, 420 /550t)		95	2	English Channel
George Mixtowe	1420–22		Falcon (BL, 80t)	59	3+	English Channel, North Sea
Nicholas Neel	1415		Paul (BL, 24t)	30	1	English Channel
Ralph Pateman	1414–16	Rodcogge (S, 120t)		25–32	6	Irish Sea, Gascony, English Channel
Edmund Pathe	1421		Edmund (BL, tonnage nk) – only ref to this 'de la Tour' vessel and master[180]	34	1	English Channel

Master	Period in royal service	Sailing ships	Oared vessels	Crew sizes	No. of known voyages	Known voyages
William Payn	**1416–22**	*Margaret* (S, 70); *Paul* (CA, 600t); *Grace Dieu* (GS, 1,400t)		**16–199**	**2+**	**Irish Sea, English Channel**
John Piers	**1415–18**	*Little Trinity* (S, 120t)		**23–33**	**3+**	**Gascony, English Channel, North Sea, the Baltic**
Walter Phelipot	c. 1421–22		*James* (BL, tonnage nk)	26	1+	English Channel
John Piers	**1415-18**	*Little Trinity* (S, 120t)		**23-33**	**3+**	**Gascony, English Channel, North Sea, the Baltic**
William Prowse or Proute	1420–c. 1421		*James* (BL, tonnage nk)	nk	1	English Channel
Henry (Hankyn) Pytman	1415–c. 1417	*Rodcogge* (S, 120t)		25	2+	English Channel, Gascony
Richard Richeman	1415		*Gabriel Harfleur* (BL, 40t)	nk	nk	nk
William Richeman	**1415–23**	*Grand Gabriel* (S, 180t); *Marie Sandwich* (CA, 550t, shipkeeping only); *George* (CA, 600t)		**71**	**5**	**Gascony, English Channel**
William Robynson	**1415–c. 1420**	*Nicholas* (S, 330t)		**44**	**3+**	**Gascony, English Channel**
Richard Rowe (retained 1421)	**c. 1416–23; c. 1435–36**		*Swan* (BL, 20t); *Valentine* (BL/ BG, 100t)	**78**	**5+**	**English Channel, North Sea**
William Russell	1413–15		*Paul* (BL, 24t)	33	2	North Sea, English Channel
Robert Shadde	**1414–22**	*Philippe* (S, 130t)	*Nicholas* (BL, 120t)	**24–133**	**16**	**North Sea, Gascony, English Channel**

Master	Period in royal service	Sailing ships	Oared vessels	Crew sizes	No. of known voyages	Known voyages
John Sibbs or Sybill	1415–c. 1417		*Gabriel Harfleur* (BL, 40t)	44	2+	English Channel
Philip Smyth	1416		*George* I (BL, 24t)	33	1	English Channel
John Sterling (cf. also Richard Yeoman)	**1420–22**		***Katherine Breton* (BL, tonnage nk)**	**10**	**2+**	**English Channel**
William Tenderley/ Tendrell	**1417–23**	***Christopher* (CA, 600t)**		**80–100**	**1+**	**Gascony**
Stephen Thomas	**1413–22**	***Thomas* (S, 160t); *Trinity Royal* (GS, 500t)**		**35–199**	**11+**	**Gascony, English Channel**
John Thornyng	1417	*Andrew* (CA, 400t)		100	nk	nk
John Utrell	1413–c. 1417	*Little Marie,* (S, 80t)		16	7+	Gascony, English Channel
Richard Walssh	**1413–20**	***Grand Marie* (S, 116t /140t)**		**27–39**	**9+**	**Gascony, Western France, English Channel**
Thomas Walssh	1413–15		*Gabriel* (BL, 30t)	39	3	English Channel, North Sea
Philip Webbe (John Bedell was also master in this period, exact dates nk)	c. 1420–22		*Marie Breton* (BG, tonnage nk)	nk	2+ possibly	English Channel
Stephen Welles	**1416–22**		***Craccher* (BL, 56t)**	**72**	**4+**	**English Channel, Gascony**
William Will	c. 1417–18	*Little Marie* (S, 80t) – sank 1418		Probably approx. 16	1	Gascony
John William	1413–22	*Rodcogge* (S, 120t); *Cog John* (S, 220t); *Jesus* (GS, 1,000t)		32–200	7+	Ireland, Irish Sea, Gascony, English Channel
William Wilton	1420–21	*Marie Breton* (S, tonnage nk)		nk	2+	North Sea, English Channel

Master	Period in royal service	Sailing ships	Oared vessels	Crew sizes	No. of known voyages	Known voyages
John Yafford	1420–22		*Roose* (BL, 30t)	30	1+	English Channel
William Yalton	*c.* **1417–22**	***Christopher Spain* (S, tonnage nk); *Trinity Royal* (GS, 500t)**	**nk**	**nk**	**1+**	
Richard Yeoman	c. 1420–22		*Katherine Breton* (BL, tonnage nk)	10	2	English Channel

APPENDIX 2[183]

Henry V's Ships

Notes

1   The names of all royal ships were suffixed by *de la Toure* (of the Tower), or some variant of the phrase.
2   Crew size: where maximum and minimum crew sizes are known, the range is given.

Grace Dieu, **great ship**[184]

Tonnage (burden): 1,400
No. of masts: 2 or 3
Max. no. of oars: –
Crew size: 199
Origin and date of acquisition: built Southampton 1416–20, John Hoggekyn (master shipwright) and Robert Berd (clerk of works).
Disposal or loss: laid up at Bursledon 1434; destroyed by fire 1439.
Summary history: biggest ship ever seen in England up to the early fifteenth century. Participated in the Earl of Devon's seakeeping voyage 1420, but the voyage ended in mutiny off the Isle of Wight. Moored in the Hamble 1420–34.

Holy Ghost, great ship

Tonnage (burden): 740/760
No. of masts: 1
Max. no. of oars: –
Crew size: 99–199
Origin and date of acquisition: originally the *Santa Clara*, a ship belonging to the Queen of Spain; captured late 1413/early 1414 by one of William Soper's ships; rebuilt at Southampton 1414–15 as the *Holy Ghost*.
Disposal or loss: docked at Bursledon 1426; last mentioned as a structure 1447–52.
Summary history: only ever used in war operations; participated in the Earl of Dorset's expedition to the Seine (1416), the battles of 1416 and 1417 (the ship was damaged in both) and the Earl of Devon's seakeeping voyage (1420). Varying tonnage figures may have been due to the addition of a summercastle and summerhutch for the Duke of Bedford's 1416 expedition.

Jesus, great ship

Tonnage (burden): 1,000
No. of masts: 2
Max. no. of oars: –
Crew size: 139–201
Origin and date of acquisition: built at Smallhythe, Kent 1415–17 by William Goodey (master shipwright).
Disposal or loss: laid up at Southampton in the 1420s; sold in derelict condition 1446.
Summary history: entered service in 1417 and most probably participated in Huntingdon's 1417 sea battle; soon after conveyed Henry V across the Channel for his second invasion of France; participated in the Earl of Devon's seakeeping voyage (1420).

Trinity Royal, great ship

Tonnage (burden): 500/540
No. of masts: 1
Max. no. of oars: –
Crew size: 200
Origin and date of acquisition: rebuilt from the old royal great ship *Trinity* (300 tons) at Greenwich, Kent 1413–15.
Disposal or loss: laid up in a dock at Hamble 1429–30; last mentioned as a structure 1439–42.
Summary history: only ever used for war operations. The ship carried Henry V to Normandy in 1415 for his first invasion of France, participated in the Earl of Dorset's 1416 expedition to the Seine and in the 1416 battle, in which it was damaged. Also took part in Huntingdon's battle off the Chef de Caux in 1417, the Earl of Devon's seakeeping voyage (1420) and was used on various voyages in the 1420–22 period, but the details of these are unclear. A summerhutch was added to the ship in 1416, which may explain the variant tonnage figures; underwent major repairs to its mast in the years 1420–22.

Christopher Spain, ship

Tonnage (burden): nk
No. of masts: 1
Max. no. of oars: –
Crew size: nk
Origin and date of acquisition: Spanish (Castilian) merchant ship captured as a prize by royal balingers commanded by Stephen Welles and Ralph Huskard, part of a seakeeping force, 1417; became a royal ship on 24 August 1417.
Disposal or loss: given to Sir John St Pee on 20 August 1419.
Summary history: kept at Southampton and in the Hamble, but does not appear to have been used.

Cog John, ship (possibly also a cog)

Tonnage (burden): 220
No. of masts: 1
Max. no. of oars: –
Crew size: 44
Origin and date of acquisition: acquired by Henry when he was Prince of Wales, before 21 March 1413; later purchased by the Crown from Roger Mynde of Bristol at the end of May 1413, for £166 13s 4d.[185]
Disposal or loss: sank off Brittany on 7 October 1414.
Summary history: there is no evidence that the *Cog John* was the same as a Prussian ship given to the Duke of Bedford in 1407, as suggested by Dr Rose, though unfortunately we do not know where it came from before Mynde had it in 1413. The vessel was the largest ship in Henry V's fleet before 1415; used on two voyages to Bordeaux for wine, and sank on the second.

Grand Gabriel, ship

Tonnage (burden): 180
No. of masts: 1
Max. no. of oars: –
Crew size: 30
Origin and date of acquisition: origin unknown, acquired by the Crown on 3 October 1415.
Disposal or loss: granted in a 'devastated' state to William Catton, clerk of the king's ships, along with the balinger *Gabriel*, on 8 August 1419.
Summary history: made a voyage to Bordeaux in the spring of 1416, returning in May of that year. Thereafter, it seems to have stayed in English waters; eventually deteriorated or suffered serious damage.

Grand Marie, ship

Tonnage (burden): 116/140
No. of masts: 1
Max. no. of oars: –
Crew size: 26–47

Origin and date of acquisition: origin unknown; acquired by the Crown on 5 December 1413.

Disposal or loss: given to Richard Buckland on 3 July 1423, in part settlement of Crown debts; valued at £200.

Summary history: undertook three cargo-carrying voyages in 1414 and 1415 (carrying pay to the Calais garrison and wine from La Rochelle and Bordeaux). It also took part in Lord Talbot's seakeeping voyage in 1415, Henry V's first invasion of France, a seakeeping patrol in 1417 with Lord Castelhon and a further voyage to Bordeaux. The lower tonnage figure was given as an estimate in 1413; the higher dates from the 1417 seakeeping voyage, and may have reflected the addition of further superstructures to the ship. It took part in the Earl of Devon's 1420 seakeeping voyage, but due to deterioration and 'sudden' breaks in the hull that occurred in the port of Hamble, the ship was taken to the River Itchen and beached on the mud there on 7 October 1420 for rebuilding. Henry V ordered the ship to be rebuilt on 24 July 1422. The work was completed in March 1423, at a cost of £182. The *Grand Marie* was one of Henry's longest-serving ships.[186]

Holy Ghost Spain, ship

Tonnage (burden): 290
No. of masts: 2
Max. no. of oars: –
Crew size: nk
Origin and date of acquisition: a Spanish prize captured in 1419 by the seakeeping patrol of Hugh Courtenay, Earl of Devon and Sir Thomas Carew.
Disposal or loss: sold for £200 to John Radcliff, Ralph Huskard, Henry Baron and John Wodefford of Southampton on 15 June 1423.
Summary history: evidently clinker-built, the ship was rebuilt and rerigged as a two-master at Southampton between 1420 and 1422 (at a cost that probably approached £400), under the supervision of the master shipwright John Hoggekyn, the man who built the *Grace Dieu*. Undertook various war voyages 1420–22 and in 1422 also went on a voyage to Bordeaux, returning on 17 January 1423.

Katherine, ship

Tonnage (burden): 210
No. of masts: 1
Max. no. of oars: –
Crew size: 60
Origin and date of acquisition: originally the *Katherine* of Guérande, Brittany; bought in January 1415 for £460; became a royal ship on 3 February 1415; possibly also known as 'the Great Hull of Brittany'.
Disposal or loss: sold for £5 in bad condition to John Pers and other Greenwich men on 6 March 1425.
Summary history: took part in Lord Talbot's seakeeping voyage and the Normandy invasion in 1415. Undertook at least three voyages to Bordeaux between 1416 and 1420; laid up on the mudflats at Greenwich in about 1420 and then docked at Deptford, evidently for repair, but no work was undertaken.

Little Marie, ship

Tonnage (burden): 80
No. of masts: 1
Max. no. of oars: –
Crew size: 17
Origin and date of acquisition: origin unknown; became a royal ship on 23 July 1413.
Disposal or loss: sank in a storm in the English Channel, 5 January 1418.[187]
Summary history: undertook at least seven voyages in royal service: five were to Bordeaux for wine cargoes, but two were war operations – Talbot's 1415 seakeeping voyage and the invasion of Normandy in the same year. It sank somewhere between Guérande and Cornwall on a return voyage from Bordeaux, loaded with wine and other goods.

Little Trinity, ship

Tonnage (burden): 120/140
No. of masts: 1
Max. no. of oars: –
Crew size: 26–36
Origin and date of acquisition: origin unknown; became a royal ship at London on 23 July 1413.
Disposal or loss: sold for £5 in bad condition to its master, John Pers, on 3 November 1418.
Summary history: sailed on ten voyages between 1413 and 1417. Seven were trading voyages: to Bordeaux (five, including an aborted voyage), Newcastle and Prussia. The latter was probably the longest voyage to a fixed destination undertaken by any of Henry's ships. The other three voyages were for war: two seakeeping patrols, Talbot (1415) and Castelhon (1417), and the 1415 invasion of Normandy. This intensive use evidently wore the ship out. The variant tonnage figures are due to the fact that the ship loaded just under 140 tons of wine on one occasion.

Margaret, ship, converted from a barge

Tonnage (burden): 70
No. of masts: 1
Max. no. of oars: –
Crew size: 17–60
Origin and date of acquisition: acquired at Beaumaris, North Wales, on 26 August 1415 and co-owned by the king and John William, one of the royal shipmasters.
Disposal or loss: sold on 31 May 1421 to Henry Lovell of Chichester for £8 3s 4d.
Summary history: apparently originally a barge, but underwent substantial rebuilding work at Beaumaris after it was acquired by the Crown, in order to turn it into a ship. The ship was used for three trading voyages to Bordeaux for wine between 1415 and 1420, and a journey to Bayonne for cables and other cordage. In 1418–19, it served in the Seine during the siege of Rouen, and was readied for a seakeeping voyage in 1419, with orders to the master to

recruit a crew of sixty. This was a very large crew for a 70-ton ship, and may suggest that it was being used under oars on this occasion.[188]

Marie Breton, ship

Tonnage (burden): 50
No. of masts: 1
Max. no. of oars: –
Crew size: 12
Origin and date of acquisition: not known, but possibly a Breton ship taken as a prize; came into royal keeping on 17 October 1415 at Sandwich, where some of the royal ships returned after the invasion of Normandy.
Disposal or loss: captured by the French off Le Crotey, 9 August 1421.
Summary history: sailed to Bordeaux in 1416, and brought back a cargo of 48 tons of wine to Tenby in south Wales. It was hired out to its master Roger Hemmyng for £10 and used in a trading voyage to Lisbon in 1417–18, returning with a cargo of wine and oil. The vessel undertook two further trading voyages in 1420–21, one of which was to Newcastle for sea coal. The *Marie Breton* was the only English royal ship to be captured by the French.

Marie Hulke, ship (possibly a hulk)

Tonnage: (burden): nk
No. of masts: 1
Max. no. of oars: –
Crew size: nk
Origin and date of acquisition: came into royal ownership on 24 June 1417 after its capture by Sir William Clifford in his voyage to Bordeaux.
Disposal or loss: sold for £5 in poor condition to men of Hamble on 1 May 1419.
Summary history: the ship was used to carry great masts from Milford Haven in Wales to Southampton, on at least one occasion.

Marie Spaniard, ship

Tonnage (burden): 100
No. of masts: 1
Max. no. of oars: –
Crew size: nk
Origin and date of acquisition: a Spanish prize ship taken by royal balingers commanded by Ralph Huskard and Stephen Welles on Lord Castelhon's seakeeping voyage, like the *Christopher Spain*; became a royal ship on 24 August 1417.
Disposal or loss: granted to Sir John Radcliffe, constable of Bordeaux Castle, 15 September 1419.
Summary history: kept at Southampton and in the Hamble; no record of any voyages.

Nicholas, ship

Tonnage (burden): 330
No. of masts: 1
Max. no. of oars: –
Crew size: 45
Origin and date of acquisition: became a royal ship on 4 May 1415 at London, where it was bought for £500.
Disposal or loss: wrecked by a storm in the Thames in May 1420; sold for £5 to John Reynold, a shipwright, in May 1424.
Summary history: underwent major internal repairs after its purchase. Took part in the 1415 invasion of Normandy, went on a voyage to Bordeaux in 1416 and made other voyages to Bordeaux between 1416 and 1420. On 1 May 1420, a storm in the Thames drove the *Nicholas* on to the mud and damaged it badly. No effort seems to have been made to repair the ship.

Philip, ship

Tonnage (burden): 130
No. of masts: 1
Max. no. of oars: –
Crew size: 25–36
Origin and date of acquisition: origin unknown; became a royal ship at Winchelsea on 9 March 1414.
Disposal or loss: sold to Robert Purfote of London for £5 on 14 October 1418.
Summary history: underwent work to strengthen its hull 1414–16. Used on four voyages between 1414 and 1416: two to Bordeaux, Talbot's seakeeping patrol and the invasion of Normandy (1415). Laid up in a dock on the Thames on 21 March 1416 because of its poor condition.

Rodcogge, ship, also known as *Flaward* of Guérande

Tonnage (burden): 120
No. of masts: 1
Max. no. of oars: –
Crew size: 26–33
Origin and date of acquisition: a ship of Breton origin in royal service from August 1413, and came into William Catton's keeping on 6 June 1414.
Disposal or loss: sold for £6 13s 4d, because of its bad condition, to Robert Colbroke of London on 3 November 1418.
Summary history: used on at least eight voyages between 1413 and 1418, of which perhaps six were to Bordeaux. On its first voyage in royal service (1413), the ship acted as a troop transport, taking John Stanley and his retinue to Dublin; in 1415, it was part of the Normandy invasion fleet.

Thomas, ship

Tonnage (burden): 160/180
No. of masts: 1
Max. no. of oars: –
Crew size: 35–50
Origin and date of acquisition: origin unknown; became a royal ship in the Thames on 22 July 1413.
Disposal or loss: sold for £133 6*s* 8*d* to a London merchant, John Church, on 5 September 1423.[187]
Summary history: one of the longest-serving of Henry's ships, the *Thomas* underwent significant repair work in Petty Wales, next to the Tower of London, between 1413 and 1416. It was used in eight Bordeaux voyages 1413–22, two of which were abandoned, the Talbot seakeeping patrol of 1415, the 1415 Normandy invasion and at least two other voyages. The *Thomas* was damaged on a voyage to Normandy in about April/May 1417, in an accident which may have killed its master, William Hore. The ship was kept in a dock at at Wapping on the Thames until 13 October 1418, when it was towed to Deptford Strand and redocked for a major rebuild, which cost just over £132. Its maintenance costs for the period 1420–22 ran into hundreds of pounds, and must have included another virtual rebuild. Why so much money was lavished on one of Henry's smaller ships is not known, but it may have been that the ship was a good sailer, and it was felt useful to preserve its hull form. In early December 1422, the *Thomas* was *en route* from Southampton to Bordeaux when its mast was broken by a storm off the Breton coast, and it put into Plymouth, where it was kept without any further repair work until it was sold.

Agase, carrack

Tonnage (burden): nk
No. of masts: 2
Max. no. of oars: –
Crew size: nk
Origin and date of acquisition: Genoese carrack captured off Netley in Southampton Water by Hugh Courtenay; became a royal ship on 7 March 1417.

Disposal or loss: smashed to pieces by a storm against the quay and walls of Southampton on 23 August 1417 and then laid up in the mud; sold to two royal shipmasters, Richard Rowe and John Bolle, for £6 13s 4d in 1418–19.
Summary history: a refurbishment attempt was cut short by the carrack's destruction.

Andrew, carrack, formerly *Galeas Negre*

Tonnage (burden): approx. 400 (800 *botte*)
No. of masts: 2
Max. no. of oars: –
Crew size: 100
Origin and date of acquisition: Genoese carrack captured in the battle off the Chef de Caux on 25 July 1417; became a royal ship on 24 August following.
Disposal or loss: sank without recovery in the port of Hamble on 15 August 1420, in a storm, due to its poor condition and the many cracks that suddenly appeared in the hull.
Summary history: order given in July 1417 to press 100 mariners for the carrack,[190] and a crew was mustered for a seakeeping voyage; otherwise, it stayed in the ports of Southampton and Hamble.

Christopher, carrack, formerly *Pynele*

Tonnage (burden): 600 (1,200 *botte*)
No. of masts: 2
Max. no. of oars: –
Crew size: 82[191]
Origin and date of acquisition: Genoese carrack captured in the battle off the Chef de Caux on 25 July 1417; became a royal ship on 24 August following.
Disposal or loss: sold to John Morgan of Bristol for £166 13s 4d on 23 May 1423.
Summary history: kept in the ports of Southampton and Hamble in the years 1417–20, though a crew was mustered on the ship for a voyage at some

time in this period; driven ashore by a storm at one point, but dug out and refloated. Extensively (and expensively) repaired and re-equipped between 1417 and 1422, and in 1422–23 was hired out to John Morgan and others for a voyage to Bordeaux. The *Christopher* was one of only two of the eight captured carracks (the other was the *George*) successfully kept in repair until the end of Henry V's reign.

George, carrack

Tonnage (burden): 600
No. of masts: 2
Max. no. of oars: –
Crew size: 100[192]
Origin and date of acquisition: Genoese carrack captured in the battle of Harfleur on 15 August 1416; became a royal ship on 10 September following.
Disposal or loss: hired out to the Venetian merchants Antonio Ungarini, Pancrazio Iustiniani and Nicholas Iustiniani 1423–25; sold to them for £133 6s 8d on 10 August 1425.
Summary history: equipped for a war voyage in 1417, and used as a guard ship at the entrance of the Hamble, 1420–21. In 1420 or 1421–22, the *George* undertook a voyage to Bordeaux and one to Bayonne.

Marie Hampton, carrack

Tonnage (burden): 500
No. of masts: 2
Max. no. of oars: –
Crew size: 90[193]
Origin and date of acquisition: Genoese carrack captured in the battle of Harfleur on 15 August 1416; became a royal ship on 10 September following.
Disposal or loss: sank at anchor in the Hamble, 13 July 1420, due to its bad condition and a storm that caused sudden cracks in the hull.
Summary history: sailed in the Carew/Castelhon/Mortimer seakeeping expedition in 1417. The carrack was one-masted when captured, but was rerigged with a mizzen sail in 1416–20.

Marie Sandwich, carrack

Tonnage (burden): 550
No. of masts: 1
Max. no. of oars: –
Crew size: nk
Origin and date of acquisition: Genoese carrack captured in the battle of Harfleur on 15 August 1416; became a royal ship on 10 September following.
Disposal or loss: sold with the carrack *Paul* as a job lot for £26 on 10 September 1424 to Richard Patyn and Richard Preste of Hamble and John and William Gladwyn of Satchell, Hampshire.
Summary history: sailed in the Carew/Castelhon/Mortimer seakeeping expedition in 1417. Laid up in the port of Hamble on 9 November 1421, because of its decay and the sudden appearance of many cracks in the hull.

Paul, carrack, formerly *Vivande*

Tonnage (burden): 600
No. of masts: 2
Max. no. of oars: –
Crew size: 100[194]
Origin and date of acquisition: Genoese carrack captured in the battle off the Chef de Caux on 25 July 1417; became a royal ship on 24 August following.
Disposal or loss: see *Marie Sandwich*, above.
Summary history: the carrack never seems to have been used, despite an order in July 1417 to press mariners for it. Stripped of most of its gear and laid up in the Hamble on 18 November 1420, because of its poor condition.

Peter, carrack

Tonnage (burden): 600 (1,200 *botte*)
No. of masts: 2
Max. no. of oars: –
Crew size: 100
Origin and date of acquisition: Genoese carrack captured in the battle off the Chef de Caux on 25 July 1417; became a royal ship on 24 August following.
Disposal or loss: sold for £13 6s 8d in poor condition to Robert Morynge and William Tassyer of Southampton, 23 October 1424.
Summary history: like the *Paul*, the *Peter* never seems to have been used, despite an order in July 1417 to press mariners for it. Kept in the ports of Southampton and Hamble; eventually docked at Southampton on 21 December 1421.

Anne, balinger

Tonnage (burden): 120
No. of masts: 2
Max. no. of oars: 68
Crew size: 62–100
Origin and date of acquisition: built at Southampton by John Hoggekyn and floated out of its building dock on 22 October 1416.
Disposal or loss: sold to John Slogge of Saltash for £30 on 27 June 1424.
Summary history: one of the three largest balingers in Henry's fleet, and the second two-master known to have been built in England (see *George* II, balinger). Took part in Castelhon's 1417 seakeeping voyage, and with the *Craccher* captured the *Christopher Spain* and *Marie Spaniard*. In autumn 1418, it was one of several vessels used to rush supplies of saltpetre and gunpowder to Caen; also involved in the 1420 Courtenay seakeeping expedition. The balinger seems to have transported the king on various occasions, as well as other VIPs.[195]

Craccher, balinger

Tonnage (burden): 56
No. of masts: 1
Max. no. of oars: 48
Crew size: 52–69
Origin and date of acquisition: given to the king on 21 September 1416 by John Hawley the Younger of Dartmouth.
Disposal or loss: sold to John Cole, Thomas Asshelden and John William of Dartmouth and Kingswear for £26 13s 4d on 30 April 1423.
Summary history: first used by Hawley as a pirate ship. In royal service, it often operated with the *Anne*. Took part in the 1417 Castelhon seakeeping voyage, and with the *Anne* captured the *Christopher Spain* and *Marie Spaniard*; also went on the same 1418 voyage as the *Anne* to Caen with a cargo of gunpowder. Docked for repairs 1420–22.

Falcon, balinger

Tonnage (burden): 80
No. of masts: 1
Max. no. of oars: 38
Crew size: 60
Origin and date of acquisition: built at Southampton as part of the retinue of the *Grace Dieu*; came into William Soper's keeping on 1 August 1420.
Disposal or loss: sold for £50 to Adam Forster of London on 1 June 1423.
Summary history: used on a number of voyages between 1420 and 1422, including the 1420 seakeeping patrol, and two voyages with cargo, one to Zeeland and one to Harfleur. It also served as a VIP transport.

Gabriel, balinger

Tonnage (burden): 30
No. of masts: 1
Max. no. of oars: 26
Crew size: 28–43
Origin and date of acquisition: may have been a balinger of the same name owned by Henry IV in 1411, though this had sixty oars; if Henry V's *Gabriel* was not this vessel, it must have been acquired between 1411 and his accession in 1413.
Disposal or loss: given to William Catton in bad condition, 8 August 1419.
Summary history: used for a variety of tasks: fishery protection in the North Sea in 1413; it was sent with the balinger *Peter* to load timber and boards at Winchelsea, Smallhythe and Newhythe for the construction of the *Trinity Royal* at Greenwich; it took part in the Talbot seakeeping voyage in 1415 and in the battle off the Chef de Caux in 1417.

Gabriel Harfleur, balinger formerly *St Gabriel de Hennebont*, ship

Tonnage (burden): 40
No. of masts: 1
Max. no. of oars: 26
Crew size: 45
Origin and date of acquisition: Breton ship captured in Lord Talbot's February–April 1415 seakeeping voyage; came into William Catton's keeping at Winchelsea on 20 October 1415.
Disposal or loss: lost at sea in the early to mid-1420s.
Summary history: the *St Gabriel* was a Breton trading vessel: although described as a 'ship', it had thirty-four oars and was reworked under William Soper's supervision in 1415 as the twenty-six-oar *Gabriel Harfleur*, at a cost of £59. It is possible that the balinger was used in the 1415 invasion of Normandy, and it certainly took part in the Earl of Dorset's voyage to Harfleur

in 1416. It was involved in Huntingdon's battle off the Chef de Caux in 1417, and at least one seakeeping patrol in 1417–18, capturing some enemy goods off Winchelsea. The balinger carried on in service into the 1420s.

George I, balinger

Tonnage (burden): 24
No. of masts: 1
Max. no. of oars: 30
Crew size: 34
Origin and date of acquisition: served between 27 January and 28 April 1416; then assigned to the defence of Harfleur.
Disposal or loss: nk
Summary history: served for three months, in the Earl of Dorset's voyage to Harfleur and the seakeeping patrol which followed it. (The two balingers called *George* were not known as 'I' and 'II' at the time: the numerals simply serve to distinguish them here.)

George II, balinger

Tonnage (burden): 120
No. of masts: 2
Max. no. of oars: 71
Crew size: 40–143
Origin and date of acquisition: built at Smallhythe, Kent, 1416 and joined the king's ships on 18 September 1416.
Disposal or loss: sold for £20 to William Bentley of Plymouth on 31 August 1423.
Summary history: the balinger was built 'in the manner of a galley'; the earliest known two-master to be built in England, completed shortly before the *Anne*. The balinger was used to carry the king between Dover and Calais on at least one occasion and took part in two or more seakeeping expeditions.

James, balinger

Tonnage (burden): nk
No. of masts: 1
Max. no. of oars: 22
Crew size: 36–40
Origin and date of acquisition: built as the follower of the great ship *Holy Ghost* at Southampton, 1414–15; operated under the name *James* by January 1416,[196] though did not feature in Catton's lists as a separate vessel until 21 March 1417.
Disposal or loss: granted to Ralph Botiller for the defence of Dieppe in June 1422.
Summary history: took part in the battle of Harfleur, 1416; carried supplies to Normandy in 1418 and 1419; part of the 1420 seakeeping patrol.

Katherine Breton, balinger

Tonnage (burden): nk
No. of masts: 1
Max. no. of oars: 8
Crew size: 11
Origin and date of acquisition: captured by the Carew/Castelhon/Mortimer seakeeping voyage, 1417; probably Breton in origin; joined the king's ship on 1 September 1417.
Disposal or loss: sold for £20 to John Starling of Greenwich on 5 March 1423.
Summary history: given its small number of oars, the *Katherine Breton* may have functioned purely as a sailing vessel; used on a wide variety of voyages 1417–22, to Normandy and around the English coast, and was used to carry victuals.

Little Jesus, balinger

Tonnage (burden): nk
No. of masts: 1
Max. no. of oars: 38

Crew size: nk
Origin and date of acquisition: built 1416–17 at Smallhythe as the follower of the great ship *Jesus.*
Disposal or loss: nk
Summary history: substantially rebuilt at Southampton 1427; rebuilt again at Bursledon as a three-master, 1435–36; eventual fate unknown.

Little John, balinger

Tonnage (burden): nk
No. of masts: 1
Max. no. of oars: 8
Crew size: 34[197]
Origin and date of acquisition: originally belonged to the Duke of Bedford and became a royal ship in about January 1416.
Disposal or loss: smashed against the walls of Southampton by a storm and sold to men of the port for £1 3s 6d in 1420.
Summary history: used to patrol the Seine Estuary around Harfleur from January to April 1416; served in Huntingdon's fleet at the battle off the Chef de Caux in 1417.

Marie, barge

Tonnage (burden): nk
No. of masts: 1
Max. no. of oars: 20
Crew size: nk
Origin and date of acquisition: built at Smallhythe 1410 and became a royal ship in August that year.
Disposal or loss: nk
Summary history: repaired at Sandwich in late May or early June 1413; sent to Lisbon with an ambassador[19] in about July 1413. No further information.

Marie Breton, barge

Tonnage (burden): nk
No. of masts: 1
Max. no. of oars: 8
Crew size: nk
Origin and date of acquisition: probably a Breton prize ship; co-owned by the king and Richard Rowe; became a royal ship on 3 February 1420.
Disposal or loss: sold because of its poor condition for £40 to John Tendryng of Dartmouth on 7 July 1422.
Summary history: used on voyages from Southampton to victual Harfleur and to carry soldiers to France, 1420–22.

Nicholas, balinger

Tonnage (burden): 120
No. of masts: 1
Max. no. of oars: 24
Crew size: 95–133
Origin and date of acquisition: built in 1417 at Ratcliffe on the Thames and became a royal ship on 30 March; appears to have been originally built for the Duke of Bedford.
Disposal or loss: sold on 11 September 1422 to John More, William Strange, Richard Rowe (*sic*) and other men of Dartmouth for £66 13s 4d.
Summary history: used for eleven voyages between 1417 and 1421, most of them seakeeping patrols, but was also used for reconnaissance and other secret purposes; part of Huntingdon's fleet in the battle off the Chef de Caux, 1417. Unusually, the inventories either have not included a large number of the balinger's oars, or it operated mainly under sail: twenty-four oars seems far too few for a balinger that could carry 133 men.[199]

Paul, balinger

Tonnage (burden): 24
No. of masts: 1
Max. no. of oars: 21
Crew size: 24–34
Origin and date of acquisition: origin not known; became a king's ship on 23 July 1413.
Disposal or loss: sunk during Lord Talbot's seakeeping expedition, February–April 1415.
Summary history: only known to have served on two voyages, a fishery protection patrol in the North Sea in 1413 and Talbot's voyage.

Peter, balinger

Tonnage (burden): 24
No. of masts: 1
Max. no. of oars: 20
Crew size: 24
Origin and date of acquisition: origin not known; became a king's ship on 24 July 1413.
Disposal or loss: granted on 16 February 1415 to Gilbert Umfraville.
Summary history: used on a fishery protection voyage in the North Sea in 1413, and also went to Sussex and Kent to load timber and boards for construction of the *Trinity Royal* in late 1413 or early 1414. It remained in the Thames from 22 March 1414.

Roose, balinger

Tonnage (burden): 30
No. of masts: 2
Max. no. of oars: 27
Crew size: 37
Origin and date of acquisition: forfeited to the Crown at Bayonne and brought back by the royal balinger masters Ralph Huskard and Stephen Welles; came into William Soper's custody on 24 February 1420.
Disposal or loss: sold for £1 6s 8d to William Castle of Southampton on 17 February 1425, because of its bad condition.
Summary history: used in various operations 1420–22, including a war voyage to Crotey and Dieppe with the balinger *James* in November 1421. The *Roose* had two guns on board when it was acquired, and was the only one of Henry V's oared vessels to carry cannon.

Swan, balinger

Tonnage (burden): 20
No. of masts: 1
Max. no. of oars: 26
Crew size: 27–36
Origin and date of acquisition: built at Greenwich between 1413 and 1415 as the follower of the *Trinity Royal*; known by the name *Swan* from at least January 1416, and listed as a vessel in its own right from 24 March 1417.
Disposal or loss: sold for £18 to John William, Thomas Downing and Nicholas Stephens of Kingswear on 17 February 1425.
Summary history: as the follower of the *Trinity Royal*, the *Swan* will have been used during the 1415 Normandy invasion, and was at the two great battles of 1416 and 1417. In 1418, the *Swan* carried letters and news for the king from England to Normandy, and from 29 September 1418 to 25 January 1419, it took part in the siege of Rouen. In 1419 and 1420, it participated in the two Courtenay seakeeping patrols; in 1421, it also helped to carry high-value royal cargoes from Southampton to Normandy. Undertook various voyages between 1420 and 1422. In October 1421, the vessel's master, Richard Rowe, was arrested, possibly for an act of piracy.[200]

Valentine, balinger and/or barge

Tonnage (burden): 100
No. of masts: 1
Max. no. of oars: 48
Crew size: 71–79
Origin and date of acquisition: built at Southampton as part of the retinue of the *Grace Dieu*, 1416–20.
Disposal or loss: sold for £80 to John Jon and John Emery of Southampton, 1 March 1424.
Summary history: used in the 1420 Courtenay seakeeping expedition, and between 1420 and 1422 served on voyages to Zeeland with cargo, to Normandy with a VIP and to Bordeaux with soldiers.

Jesus Maria, galley

Tonnage (burden): nk
No. of masts: 1
Max. no. of oars: 252
Crew size: nk
Origin and date of acquisition: built *c.* 1412 for Henry IV.
Disposal or loss: laid up on the Thames by 1413; abandoned 1415 and sold as a derelict for £13 6s 8d in 1417.
Summary history: a Mediterranean-style galley built to convey Henry IV to the Holy Land; never used. Laid up at Ratcliffe and finally abandoned in August 1415 as it was filling with water at every high tide.

Vessels of uncertain ownership or use

Edmund de la Toure, balinger

Tonnage (burden): nk
No. of masts: nk
Max. no. of oars: nk
Crew size: 35
Origin and date of acquisition: nk
Disposal or loss: nk
Summary history: described as 'a balinger of the king' and given the suffix
de la Toure in a 24 June 1421 order to the balinger's master, Edmund Pathe,
to press thirty-four mariners for the vessel and to bring it to Normandy as
soon as possible 'for certain business of the king'. No further references have
been found for this vessel.[201]

Unnamed great ship at Bayonne

Tonnage (burden): nk, but 1,100+?
No. of masts: nk
Max. no. of oars: nk
Crew size: nk
Origin and date of acquisition: construction possibly ordered 1416.
Disposal or loss: possibly not completed.
Summary history: perhaps one of two ships ordered by Henry V on
4 September 1416, to be built at Bayonne. It was described in extraordinary
detail in a letter from John Alcetre at Bayonne on 25 April 1419. The keel
was 112ft (34.1m) in length, the widest beam was 46ft (14m) across and from
stempost to sternpost the vessel measured 186ft (56.7m). Thirty-six strakes
of planking had been assembled, and eleven beams inserted, but the keel
had rotted and needed changing. Alcetre reckoned it would not be ready
for four or five years. The ship must have been of over 1,000 tons burden,
but removing the keel from a structure this size would have been impossible
without breaking up the hull, and this may explain why nothing more is
heard of the ship.[202]

APPENDIX 3

The Royal Ships 22 July 1413–28 April 1416: Total Time in Service, Time at Sea and Repair/Maintenance Costs

Ship	Type	Tonnage	Total days in royal ownership over period	Total days at sea over period	Repair and maintenance costs over period (£)	Percentage of total time at sea
Holy Ghost	great ship	700	167	92	Not separated	55
Trinity Royal	great ship	500	406	197	Not separated	48.5
Cog John	ship	220	446	249	114	55.8
Grand Gabriel	ship	180	231	134	39	58
Grand Marie	ship	116/140	825	447	97	54
Katherine	ship	210	484	289	99	59.7
Little Marie	ship	80	1,056	629	58	59.6
Little Trinity	ship	120	1,082	712	83	65.8
Margaret	ship	70	281	245	61	87.1
Marie Breton	ship	50	218	136	7	62.4
Nicholas	ship	330	367	234	75	63.8
Philip	ship	130	736	442	87	60
Rodcogge	ship	120	709	475	114	67
Thomas	ship	180	1,056	698	120	66.1
Gabriel	balinger	30	628	230	30	36.6
Gabriel Harfleur	balinger	40	191	92	59	48.2

Ship	Type	Tonnage	Total days in royal ownership over period	Total days at sea over period	Repair and maintenance costs over period (£)	Percentage of total time at sea
George I	balinger	24	92	92	59	100
*Paul**	balinger	24	626	78	12	12.5
*Peter***	balinger	24	656	29	8	4.4

* 114 days unaccounted for in the pay records: if these were days at sea, the time at sea would rise to 20.1 per cent.

** 144 days unaccounted for in the pay records: if these were days at sea, the time at sea would rise to 23.2 per cent.[203]

APPENDIX 4

Major Types of Weapons: Maximum Armaments Recorded

Ship and type	Date	Guns and chambers	Bows and arrows (sheaves)	Crossbows and bolts	Gads/ darts for the top	Other hand weapons	Grapnels
Grace Dieu GS	1420	3+3	40+50	-	144	-	1
Holy Ghost GS	1416	7+12	14+91	6	102	63	2
Jesus GS	1422	2+1	-	-	-	-	-
Trinity Royal GS	1420	5+8	-	8+360	120	22	1
Christopher Spain S	1417–19	-	-	-	-	-	-
Cog John S	-	-	-	-	48 darts	20	-
Grand Gabriel S	1415–19	-	-	-	-	-	-
Grand Marie S	1413	3+10	21+25	-	30 gads + 48 darts	15	1
Holy Ghost Spain S	1419	2+6	-	-	-	-	1 (acquired 1420–22)
Katherine S	1416	2 guns	-	-	48 darts	4	1
Little Marie S	1416	-	8+10	-	-	2	-
Little Trinity S	1416	20 gunstones (1413)	8+12	-	132 darts (1413)	12 (1413)	-
Margaret S	1415–21	-	-	-	-	-	-
Marie Breton S	1421	-	8+10	-	-	5	-

Ship and type	Date	Guns and chambers	Bows and arrows (sheaves)	Crossbows and bolts	Gads/ darts for the top	Other hand weapons	Grapnels
Marie Hulke S	1417–19	-	-	-	-	-	-
Marie Spaniard S	1417	-	-	-	-	-	1 (small)
Nicholas S	1416	-	-	-	-	-	1
Philip S	1414–18	-	-	-	-	-	-
Rodcogge S	1414	1	-	-	48 darts	-	-
Thomas S	1413	4+12	11+24	-	16 gads + 144 darts	23	1
Andrew CA	1417-20	-	-	-	-	-	-
Agase CA	1417	-	-	-	-	-	-
Christopher CA	1417	2+4	-	-	-	-	-
George CA	1417	3+6	40+111	-	-	-	-
Marie Hampton CA	1416	-	-	-	-	-	1
Marie Sandwich CA	1416	-	-	-	-	-	1
Paul CA	1417	3+1	-	-	-	-	1
Peter CA	1417	3+4	-	-	-	-	1
Anne BL	1420	-	12+20	-	-	-	1
Craccher BL	1420	-	12+30	-	-	1	-
Falcon BL	1420	-	20+20	-	-	-	-
Gabriel BL	1413–19	-	-	-	-	-	-
Gabriel Harfleur BL	1420	-	12+12	-	-	-	-
George I BL	1416	-	-	-	-	-	-
George II BL	1420	-	supplied with 20 bowstrings	-	-	-	-
James BL	1420	-	12+12	-	-	-	-
Katherine Breton BL	1422	-	-	-	36 darts	-	-
Little John BL	1416–22	-	-	-	-	-	-
Marie Breton BG	1420	-	-	-	36 darts	8	-
Nicholas BL	1420	-	10+20	-	-	-	-
Paul BL	1413	-	7+15	-	-	2	-
Peter BL	1413	-	?+7	-	4	-	-

APPENDIX 4

Ship and type	Date	Guns and chambers	Bows and arrows (sheaves)	Crossbows and bolts	Gads/ darts for the top	Other hand weapons	Grapnels
Roose BL	1420	2+2	-	-	-	-	-
Swan BL	1420	-	12+12	-	-	-	-
Valentine BL/ BG	1420	-	20+20	-	-	-	-

ABBREVIATIONS IN SOURCES

CCR	*Calendar of Close Rolls*
CIM	*Calendar of Inquisitions Miscellaneous*
CPR	*Calendar of Patent Rolls*
CSP Ven	*Calendar of State Papers, Venetian*
MM	*Mariner's Mirror*
OED	Oxford English Dictionary, via www.oed.com
RF	Rymer's *Foedora* (followed by volume number), ed. T. Rymer, London, 1739–45, via www.british-history. ac.uk/rymer-foedera/

Documentary Sources

The National Archives, Kew

E101 Exchequer, Accounts Various
E364 Exchequer, Foreign Accounts
E403 Exchequer of Receipt, Issue Rolls
C47 Chancery Miscellanea
SC8 Special Collections: Ancient Petitions

Cornwall Record Office

Cornwall Record Office AR/22/5, via http://discovery.nationalarchives.gov.uk

Staffordshire Record Office

D.641.3, Cossey 16, temp no 479

Wiltshire and Swindon History Centre

Earl of Radnor MS 490/1547

BIBLIOGRAPHY

Alertz, U., 'The naval architecture and oar systems of medieval and later galleys', in Morrison 1995, pp.142–62.

Allmand, C.T., *Henry V*, London, 1992.

Anderson, R. and R.C., *The Sailing-Ship: Six Thousand Years of History*, London, 1926.

Anderson, R.C., 'The Bursledon Ship', *MM* 20 (1934), pp.154–70.

Anderson, R.C., *Oared Fighting Ships from Classical Times to the Coming of Steam*, Kings Langley, 1976.

Bailey, M. and S.H. Rigby (eds), *Town and Country in the Age of the Black Death: Essays in Honour of John Hatcher*, Turnhout, 2012.

Balard, M. and C. Picard, *La Méditeranée au Moyen Age*, Paris, 2014.

Bange, B., 'The Caravel', in Bennett 2009, pp.84–98.

Bartlett, C., *The English Longbowman 1330–1515*, Oxford, 1995.

Bellaguet, M.L. (trans.), *Chronique du Religieux de Saint-Denys, Contenant Le Règne de Charles VI, de 1380 à 1422*, Paris, 1844.

Bennett, J. (ed.), *Sailing into the Past: Learning from Replica Ships*, London, 2009.

Bennett, M., *Agincourt 1415: Triumph against the Odds*, Oxford, 1991.

Bolton, J.L., *The Medieval English Economy 1150–1500*, London, 1980.

Bondioli, M., R. Burlet and A. Zysberg, 'Oar mechanics and oar power in medieval and later galleys', in Morrison 1995, pp.172–205.

Burwash, D., *English Merchant Shipping 1460–1540*, Newton Abbot, 1969.

Carpenter Turner, W.J., 'The building of the *Gracedieu*, *Valentine* and *Falconer* at Southampton, 1416–20', *MM* 40 (1954), pp.55–72.

Casson, L., 'Merchant galleys', in Morrison 1995, pp.127–41.

Channel Pilot: Isles of Scilly and South Coast of England, from Cape Cornwall to Bognor Regis, and North-west and North Coasts of France from Pointe de Penmarc'h to Cap d'Antifer, London, 1996.

Chun, D., *The River Hamble: A History*, Stroud, 2014.

Clark, L. (ed.), *The Fifteenth Century VII: Conflicts, Consequences and the Crown in the Late Middle Ages*, Woodbridge, 2007.

Corbett, J.S. (ed.), *Fighting Instructions 1530–1816*, Navy Records Society Vol. 29, London, 1925.

Crumlin-Pedersen, O., *Archaeology and the Sea in Scandinavia and Britain*, Maritime Culture of the North 3, Roskilde, 2010.

Curry, A., 'English Armies in the Fifteenth Century', in Curry and Hughes 1994, pp.39–68.

—, 'After Agincourt, What Next? Henry V and the Campaign of 1416', in Clark 2007, pp.23–51.

—, 'Carew, Sir Thomas (1368?–1431)', *Oxford Dictionary of National Biography*, Oxford University Press, 2008.

—, *The Battle of Agincourt: Sources and Interpretations*, Woodbridge, 2009.

—, and M. Hughes (eds), *Arms, Armies and Fortifications in the Hundred Years War*, Woodbridge, 1994.

De la Roncière, C., *Histoire de La Marine Française*, Vol. II, Paris, 1900.

De Meer, S., 'The Nao of Mataro: A Medieval Ship Model', n.d., www.iemed.org/dossiers-en/dossiers-iemed/accio-cultural/ mediterraneum-1/documentacio/anau.pdf

Denis, L., *Atlas topographique de l'ancienne province de Normandie et pays limitrophes*, revised H. Brué, Paris, 1817.

Dobbs, C., 'The Galley' in Marsden 2009, pp.124–35.

Dodd, G. (ed.), *Henry V: New Interpretations*, Woodbridge, 2013.

Dodds, J. and J. Moore, *Building the Wooden Fighting Ship*, London, 1984.

Duffy, M., S, Fisher, B. Greenhill, D.J. Starkey and J. Youings (eds), *The New Maritime History of Devon. Volume I: From Early Times to the Late Eighteenth Century*, London, 1992.

Dyer, A., *Decline and Growth in English Towns 1400–1600*, London, 1991.

Eddison, J., *Medieval Pirates. Pirates, Raiders and Privateers 1204–1453*, Stroud, 2013.

Ellis, F. (ed.), *The Chronicle of John Hardyng*, London, 1812.

Ellis, H., *Original Letters Illustrative of English History*, Second Series, Vol. 1, London, 1827.

Farmer, D.H., *The Oxford Dictionary of Saints*, Oxford, 1978.

Fowler, K. (ed.), *The Hundred Years War*, London, 1971.

Friel, I., 'Documentary Sources and the Medieval Ship', *International Journal of Nautical Archaeology*, 12 (1983), pp.41–62.

—, 'Henry V's Grace Dieu and the Wreck in the R. Hamble near Bursledon, Hampshire, *International Journal of Nautical Archaeology*, 22 (1993), pp.3–19.

—, 'The Carrack: The Advent of the Full Rigged Ship', in Unger 1994, pp.77–90.

—, *The Good Ship. Ships, Shipbuilding and Technology in England 1200–1520*, London and Baltimore, 1995.

—, *The British Museum Maritime History of Britain and Ireland c. 400–2001*, London, 2003.

—, 'How Much Did the Sea Matter in Medieval England (*c.* 1200–*c.* 1500)?', in Gorski 2012, pp.167–85.

—, '1295: The Year of the Galleys', lecture, 31 October 2013, Gresham College, London: www.gresham.ac.uk/lectures-and-events/1295-the-year-of-the-galleys.

—, 'The Rise and Fall of the Big Ship, 1400–1520', in E. Jones (ed.), *The World of the Newport Ship* (forthcoming).

Gairdner, J. (ed.), *The Historical Collections of a Citizen of London in the Fifteenth Century*, Camden Society, New Series Vol. 17, London, 1876.

— (ed.), *Sailing Directions for the Circumnavigation of England and for a Voyage to the Straights of Gibraltar*, Hakluyt Society, First Series, Vol. LXXIX, London, 1889.

— (ed.) *The Paston Letters*, Vols 1–6 (microprint edition), Gloucester, 1983.

Gardiner, D.M. (ed.), *A Calendar of Early Chancery Proceedings Relating to West Country Shipping*, Devon and Cornwall Record Society, Vol. 21, Torquay, 1976.

Given-Wilson, C., P. Brand, S. Phillips, M. Ormrod, G. Martin, A. Curry and R. Horrox (eds), *Parliament Rolls of Medieval England*, Woodbridge, 2005.

Gorski, R. (ed.), *Roles of the Sea in Medieval England*, Woodbridge, 2012.

Guilmartin, J., *Gunpowder and Galleys: Changing Technology and Mediterranean Warfare at Sea in the Sixteenth Century*, Cambridge, 1974.

Hardy, R., 'Historical Importance and Assessment of the Longbow Assemblage' and 'Longbows', in Hildred 2011, pp.586–94.

—, *Longbow. A Social and Military History*, Yeovil, 2012.

— et al., 'Assessment of the Working Capabilities of the Longbows', in Hildred 2011, pp.622–32.

Hardy, T.D. (ed.), *Rotuli Normanniae in Turri Londiniensi Asservati, Johanne et Henrico Quinto Angliae Regibus*, London, 1835.

Hatcher, J., *Plague, Population and the English Economy 1348–1530*, London, 1977.

Hattendorf, J.B., R.J.B. Knight, A.W.H. Pearsall, N.A.M. Rodger and G. Till (eds), *British Naval Documents 1204–1960*, Navy Records Society, London, 1993.

Hildred, A. (ed.), *Weapons of Warre: The Armaments of the Mary Rose* (Archaeology of the Mary Rose: Vol. 3), Portsmouth, 2011.

Hoheisel, W.-D., 'The Hanseatic Cog', in Bennett 2009, pp.70–83.

Holland, A.J., *Ships of British Oak: The Rise and Decline of Wooden Shipbuilding in Hampshire*, Newton Abbot, 1971.

Hoskins, P. and A. Curry, *Agincourt 1415: A Tourist's Guide to the Campaign*, Barnsley, 2014.

Hughes, M., 'The Fourteenth-century French Raids on Hampshire and the Isle of Wight', in Curry and Hughes 1994, pp.121–43.

Hutchinson, G., *Medieval Ships and Shipping*, London and Washington, 1997.

International Congress of Maritime Museums, *Fourth Conference Proceedings*, Paris, 1983.

Johansen, R., 'The Viking Ships of Skuldelev', in Bennett 2009, pp.52–69.

Kenyon, J.R., 'Coastal Artillery Fortification in England in the Late Fourteenth and Early Fifteenth Centuries', in Curry and Hughes 1994, pp.145–49.

Kingsford, C.L., 'West Country Piracy: The School of English Seamen', in C.L. Kingsford, *Prejudice and Promise in 15th Century England*, Oxford, 1925, pp.78–106.

Kowaleski, M., 'The Port Towns of Fourteenth-century Devon', in Duffy et al. 1992, pp.62–71.

—, 'The Demography of Maritime Communities in Late Medieval England', in Bailey and Rigby 2012, pp.87–118.

La Barre, A., *The French Coasting Pilot; being a description of every harbour, roadsted, channel, cove, and river on the French coast in the English Channel and in the Bay of Biscay … ,* Plymouth, 1825.

Lambert. C., *Shipping the Medieval Military: English Maritime Logistics in the Fourteenth Century*, Woodbridge, 2011.

Lane F.C., 'Tonnages, Medieval and Modern', *Economic History Review*, Second Series Vol. XVII (1964), pp.213–33.

McGlynn, S., *By Sword and Fire: Cruelty and Atrocity in Medieval Warfare*, London, 2008.

McGrail, S. (ed.), *Medieval Ships and Harbours of Northern Europe*, BAR International Series 66, Oxford, 1979.

—, *Boats of the World from the Stone Age to Medieval Times*, Oxford, 2001.

—, *Early Ships and Seafaring: Water Transport within Europe*, Barnsley, 2014.

McHardy, A.K., 'Religion, Court Culture and Propaganda: The Chapel Royal in the Reign of Henry V', in Dodd 2013, pp.131–56.

Mackman, J. and M. Stevens (eds), *Court of Common Pleas: The National Archives Cp 40 1399–1500*, London, 2010.

Marsden, P., 'Interpretation of the Decks', in *Mary Rose Your Noblest Shipp: Anatomy of a Tudor Warship*, Archaeology of the Mary Rose Vol. 2, Portsmouth, 2009, pp.371–78.

Marsden, R.G. (ed.), *Documents Relating to the Law and Custom of the Sea Vol. I: A.D. 1205–1648*, Navy Records Society Vol. 49, London, 1915.

Morosini, A. (ed.), *Chronique D'Antonio Morosini. Extraits Relatifs à l'Histoire de France. Tome Deuxième 1414–1428*, Paris, 1899 (cited as Morosini 1899).

Morrison, J., *Long Ships and Round Ships: Warfare and Trade in the Mediterranean 3000 BC–500 AD*, National Maritime 'The Ship' Series, London, 1980.

— (ed.), *The Age of the Galley. Mediterranean Oared Vessels since Pre-classical Times*, Conway's History of the Ship, London, 1995.

Mortimer, I., *1415: Henry V's Year of Glory*, London, 2010.

Nicholas, N.H., *A History of the Royal Navy from the Earliest Times to the Wars of the French Revolution*, 2 Volumes, London, 1847.

Osborne, M., *Defending Hampshire: The Military Landscape from Prehistory to the Present*, Stroud, 2011.

Pitcaithly, M., 'Piracy and Anglo-Hanseatic Relations, 1385–1420', in Gorski 2012, pp.125–45.

Platt, C., *Medieval Southampton: The Port and Trading Community, A.D. 1000–1600*, London, 1973.

Plets, R.M.K., J.K. Dix, J.R. Adams, J.M. Bull, T.J. Henstock, M. Gutowski and A.I. Best, 'The Use of a High-resolution 3D Chirp Sub-bottom Profiler for the Reconstruction of the Shallow Water Archaeological Site of the *Grace Dieu* (1439), River Hamble, UK', *Journal of Archaeological Science*, 36 (2009), pp.408–18.

Pratt, M., *Winchelsea: The Tale of a Medieval Town*, Bexhill, 2005.

Prynne, M.W., 'Henry V's *Grace Dieu*', *MM* 54 (1968), pp.115–28.

—, 'The Dimensions of the *Grace Dieu*', *MM* 63 (1977), pp.6–7.

Rackham, O., *The History of the Countryside*, London, 1987.

Reinders, H.R., 'Medieval Ships: Recent Finds from the Netherlands', in McGrail 1979, pp.41–3.

Richmond, C.F., 'The War at Sea', in Fowler 1971, pp.96–121.

Robinson, F.N. (ed.), *The Complete Works of Geoffrey Chaucer*, Oxford, 1974.

Rodger, N.A.M., *The Safeguard of the Sea: A Naval History of Britain. Volume One: 660–1649*, London, 1997.

—, 'Fighting the Ship: Historical Evidence', in Hildred 2011, pp.851–55.

Rose, S., 'Henry V's *Grace Dieu* and Mutiny at Sea: Some New Evidence', *MM* 63 (1977), pp.3–6.

—, *The Navy of the Lancastrian Kings: Accounts and Inventories of William Soper, Keeper of the King's Ships, 1422–1427*, Navy Records Society Vol. 123, London, 1982.

—, *Medieval Naval Warfare, 1000–1500*, London, 2002.

—, 'Pay, Henry (*d.* 1419)', *Oxford Dictionary of National Biography*, Oxford University Press, 2007.

—, 'Hawley, John, the Elder (*c.* 1350–1408)', *Oxford Dictionary of National Biography*, Oxford University Press, 2008.

—, *The Wine Trade in Medieval Europe 1000–1500*, London, 2011.

—, *England's Medieval Navy 1066–1509: Ships, Men & Warfare*, London, 2013.

Roskell, J.S., L. Clark and C. Rawcliffe (eds), *The History of Parliament: The House of Commons 1386–1421*, Woodbridge, 1993.

Sandahl, B. *Middle English Sea Terms*, Vol. 1, Uppsala, 1951.

—, *Middle English Sea Terms*, Vol. 2, Uppsala, 1958.

—, *Middle English Sea Terms*, Vol. 3, Uppsala, 1992.

Sayers, W., 'Fourteenth-century English Balingers: Whence the Name?', *MM* 93 (2007), pp.4–15.

Sherborne, J.W., 'English Barges and Balingers of the Late Fourteenth Century', *MM* 63 (1997), pp.109–14.

Sobecki, S.I., *The Sea and Medieval English Literature*, Cambridge, 2008.

Stevenson, J. (ed.), *Letters and Papers Illustrative of the Wars of the English in France in the Reign of Henry the Sixth*, Vol. 1, London, 1861.

Taylor, F. (ed.), 'The Chronicle of John Strecche for the Reign of Henry V (1414–1422)', *Bulletin of the John Rylands Library* 16 (1932), pp.3–53.

— and J.S. Roskell (eds), *Gesta Henrici Quinti: The Deeds of Henry V*, Oxford, 1975.

Taylor, J., W.R. Childs and L. Watkiss, *The St Albans Chronicle: The Chronica Maiora of Thomas Walsingham. Vol. II, 1399–1422*, Oxford, 2011.

Unger, R.W. (ed.), *Cogs, Caravels and Galleons: The Sailing Ship 1000–1600*, London, 1994.

van der Merwe, P., '*Coche seu Nave* and Carracks in the Later 14th Century', International Congress of Maritime Museums, 1983, pp.122–29.

Walker, E.B., 'The Town and Port of New Romney', *Archaeologia Cantiana* 13 (1880), pp.201–15.

Ward, R., *The World of the Medieval Shipmaster: Law, Business and the Sea, c. 1350–1450*, Woodbridge, 2009.

Williams, B. (ed.), *Henrici Quinti Anglia Regis Gesta cum Chronica Neustriae*, London, 1850.

Wright, A.P.M. and L.S. Woodger, 'Catton, William (d. 1431), of Winchelsea, Sussex', in Roskell, Clark and Rawcliffe 1993.

Wright, T. (ed.), *Political Poems and Songs Relating to English History*, Vol. II, London, 1861.

Wylie, J.H., *The Reign of Henry V. Volume I (1413–1415)*, Cambridge, 1914.

—, *The Reign of Henry V. Volume II (1415)*, Cambridge, 1919.

— and W.T. Waugh, *The Reign of Henry V. Volume III (1415–1422)*, Cambridge, 1929.

ENDNOTES

1   Lane, 1964.

2   Taylor and Roskell, 1975, pp.20–3; Allmand, 1992, chs 4–8; Rodger, 1997, pp.117–30; The National Archives (TNA), Exchequer, Lord Treasurer's Remembrancer, Foreign Accounts E364/54 and E364/59, *passim*; Friel, 1993; *Trinity Royal*: TNA E364/54, H m 1v; Lambert, 2011, p.139; Dyer, 1991, pp.13–14; Curry, 1994, p.45; horses: Allmand 1992, p.215; royal ships in 1415 fleet: TNA E364/54, E m 1v–F.

3   Allmand, 1992, pp.36–38; this brief survey of Henry's career is based on a range of sources, chiefly Allmand's indispensable biography of the king, Mortimer, 2010, and the works of Wylie and Waugh, but interpretations are my own.

4   Taylor and Roskell, 1975, pp.122–5.

5   McGlynn, 2008, pp.193–4.

6   Given-Wilson et al., 2005, 'Henry V: May 1421', 22 and Appendix 7.

7   Rodger, 1997, pp.114–16, 454–5; CCR 1405–1409, pp.59–60, 93–4.

8   This section is based on the following accounts of the clerks of the king's ships for Henry IV: TNA E101/42/39, E101/43/6, E101/43/7, E101/44/9, E101/44/11, E101/44/17 and E364/43 D m 2r–E m 1r.

9   Mortimer, 2010, p.19.

10 Rodger, 1997, pp.149, 504–9.

11 Nicolas, 1847, p.386.

12 Given-Wilson *et al.*, 2005, 'Henry V: March 1416', VIII.31; CCR 1413–19, p.525–6.

13 Friel, 2012, pp.169–75; Bolton, 1980, pp.136, 152–5, 174–5, 178–89, 193–5, 287–8, 308–9, 315–17, 327, 349.

14 TNA Exchequer, Bordeaux Constable's Accounts, E101/163/1 (1308–09), E101/173/4 (1355–58), E101/182/6 (1378–79), E101/182/2 (1359–61), E101/179/10 (1372–73); E101/183/11 (1385–86), E101/185/11 (1402–03), E101/184/19 (1409–10), E101/185/7 (1412–13), E101/191/3 (1431). I owe the transcripts of these accounts to the kindness of Professor Wendy Childs, though the conclusions drawn from them are my own responsibility.

15 Friel, forthcoming; TNA E101/185/11, E101/184/19 and E101/185/7; Ward, 2009, ch. 3.

16 TNA E364/59, H m 2r and m 1v; Rodger 1997, pp.141, 454; Lambert, 2011, pp.11–51, 202 n. 196; TNA E101/48/23; 1417 fleet: Hardy, 1835, pp.320–9; Burwash, 1969, pp.120–8; information on ship arrests: CCR 1413–19, pp.10, 19, 30, 68, 162, 165, 278, 292, 301, 310, 331, 339, 340, 343, 364, 391, 392, 395, 397, 398, 418, 428, 429; CCR 1419–22, pp.141–2, 245; CPR 1413–16, p.293; CPR 1416–22, pp.70, 71, 73, 199–200, 267, 274, 275, 329, 420; RF 9, pp.216, 218, 792–3; RF10, p.256; E403/623, mm 3 and 14; E403/624, mm 1, 3 and 15; E403/628, mm 9–14; E403/635, mm 14 and 19; E403/637, mm 4, 8 and 15; E403/641, m 5.

17 Hatcher, 1977; Bolton, 1980, pp.45–81; Dyer, 1991, pp.13–14.

18 Rose, 2013, pp.49, 61–2; Lambert, 2011, pp.139–40; Kowaleski, 2012, p.95.

19 Curry, 2009, pp.11–13; Taylor and Roskell, 1975, pp.20–1.

20 Curry, 1994, pp.44–5; Burwash, 1969, pp.90–1; Lane, 1964, pp.218–19; Rose, 2011, ch. 4.

21 E364/54 D m 2v–F m 2v; Rodger, 1997, pp.138–42; Rose, 1982, p.47.

22 Mortimer, 2010, pp.105–6, 139–40, 191, 226, 581 n. 83; Wylie and Waugh, 1914, p.449; TNA E101/48/15 and C47/28/7/30 (draft commission for Clitherowe and Curteis, 4 April 1415).

23 E403/624, mm 1–2; Hardy, 1835, pp.320–5; TNA E101/48/18 and E101/48/21.

24 TNA E403/624, m 2; E364/59, H mm 1r–2r.

25 Wylie and Waugh, 1929, p.128; TNA E364/61, G m 1v and I m 2r.

26 TNA E364/59, H m1 r, H m 1v and J m 2v; E364/61 G m 2v; E101/49/29, m 1; CSP Ven 1202–1509, Vol. 1, 1411–20, nos 214–18, via www.british-history.ac.uk/cal-state-papers/venice/vol1/pp52-61; TNA SC 8/198/9868; Wylie and Waugh, 1929, p.288.

27 Rose, 1982, pp.6–27, 34, 230–3; Pratt, 2005, p.126; Wright and Woodger, 1993; Carpenter-Turner, 1954, pp.56–8; Friel, 1993, p.4.

28 The accounts are: TNA E364/54, E364/57, E364/59 and E364/61; Friel, 1983, pp.42–51; TNA E101/44/17, m 11; E364/54, F m 2v; Rose, 1982, p.135.

29 Rose, 1982, pp.52–3; TNA E364/59, H m1r.

30 Rose, 2013, pp.47–50.

31 TNA E403/624, m1; TNA E364/59 F m 2r; Rose, 1982, p.39.

32 TNA E364/54, D m 2r–F m 2v, *passim*.

33 TNA E364/54 G m 1r; TNA E364/61 L m 2v; E364/59, H m 1r; TNA E364/57 I m 1r–m 1v; E101/49/29 m 6.

34 TNA E364/54, E364/59 and E364/61, *passim*; Rose, 1982, p.106.

35 Rose, 1982, p.38; TNA E364/59 F m 1v; Wright and Woodger, 1993.

36   Rose, 1982, pp.6–27, 230–1.

37   TNA E364/54, E m 2r; TNA E403/637, m 4.

38   Kowaleski, 1992, p.68; Kowaleski, 2012; Eddison, pp.122–53; Rodger, 1997, pp.114–15, 149.

39   TNA E101/55/12; E101/695/41: The National Archives tentatively dates this document to the reign of Henry VI (1422–71), but the master's name and crew size match those of Henry V's *Gabriel Harfleur*.

40   Rose, 1982, p.7; Mackman and Stevens, 2010: CP 40/658, rot 38 d (via www.british-history.ac.uk).

41   TNA E364/54, D m 2v and F m 2v; Rose 1982, pp.245, 275 n. 337; CPR 1416–22, p.182; TNA E101/48/26.

42   Rose, 1982, pp.42–3, 242; Corporation of London Record Office (via www.discovery.nationalarchives.gov.uk) CLA/007/EM/02/E/015, CLA/007/EM/02/H/001, CLA/007/EM/02/E/015 and CLA/007/EM/02/H/008; TNA SC 8/138/6879, CLA/007/EM/02/H/044 CLA/007/EM/02/H/044 and CLA/007/EM/02/H/036.

43   Rodger, 1997, p.115; Robinson, 1974, pp.21, 660–1.

44   Rose, 1982, pp.81, 233; CIM 1399–1422, p.330.

45   TNA E364/54, E m 2r; Robertson, 1974, p.21; Gairdner, 1889; Ward, 2009, ch. 6 gives a detailed account of the nature of both theoretical and practical navigation in late medieval northern Europe; TNA E101/53/5, ff 10 r and 38v.

46   TNA E364/54, E364/59 and E364/61, *passim*; ship's bell: TNA E364/61, I m 1r.

47   Ward, 2009, chs 3–7; Robinson, 1974, *loc. cit.*; Gairdner, 1889, p.12; TNA E101/185/7.

48   CPR 1416–22, pp.120–1, 379; Rodger, 1997, pp.147, 498–9.

49   TNA E101/48/14; E403/637, mm 10–11; Friel, 2003, pp.102–3; Ward, 2009, pp.118–21; Rose, 1982, p.47; Staffordshire County Record Office D.641.3, Cossey 16, temp no. 479: I owe a transcript of this document and the details of Morley to Professor Colin Richmond; E101/53/5, f 9v.

50   Mortimer, 2010, pp.25–6; CPR 1416–22, p.387; Hardy, 1835 pp.325–9.

51   Farmer, 1978, pp.292–3; CPR 1416–22, pp.120–1.

52   Mortimer, 2010, p 47.

53   Mortimer, 2010 pp.82–3, 97; ship decoration and flags: TNA E364/54, E364/59, E364/61 *passim*.

54   Rose, 2013, p.49; TNA E364/61, G m 1v and M m 1r.

55   OED under 'pavise', n.; TNA E364/61, J m 2r.

56   Rodger, 1997, pp.78–9, 128.

57   Marsden, 1895, p.53; Walker, 1880, p.208; C Inq Misc 1399–1422, pp.312–13; TNA SC/8/332/15762; SC 8/332/15765, 1415–22.

58   Kingsford, 1925; Rose, 2007 and 2008.

59   TNA E101/71/2/812.

60   TNA E101/48/14.

61   Bennett, 1991, pp.20–8.

62   Bennett, 1991, pp.20–4.

63   Curry, 2007, pp.36–7

64   TNA E364/54, D m 2v–F m 2v.

65   TNA E101/48/12.

66   This section is based on: Crumlin-Pedersen, 2010, pp.41–4; TNA E364/54, G m 2v; Friel, 1993, pp.4–5; Hutchinson, 1997, ch. 1 and p.32; Rose, 1982, pp.72–7, 222–4, 234; Dodds and Moore, 1984, pp.13–14, 23–4; Rackham, 1987, pp.90–1; Friel, 1995, pp.39–48, 68–76, 95–8, 204; McGrail, 2001, pp.224–6; Friel, 2013; Sandahl, 1951, pp.49–50, 52–3, 91, 111; CPR 1416–22, p.379; Friel, 1995, pp.39–46; Carpenter Turner, 1954, pp.65–6.

67   Notes for these two sections: TNA E364/61, L m 2v; Friel, 1995, pp.79–81, 148–50; Rose, 1982, pp.217–21; TNA E364/59, I m 2v; TNA E364/54 D, m 2v; Sandahl, 1951, pp.197–8; Marsden, 2009; Anderson, 1927, pp.91–6; Dobbs, 2009; Friel, 1993, p.6; TNA E364/54D, m 2r; TNA E364/61, G m 2v, L m 2v; TNA E364/54, D m 1r; TNA E364/59, G m 2r and 2v and H m 1r; E101/48/14; E101/44/17, m 8; E364/54 D m 1v.

68   This section is based on: Friel, 1995, pp.84–109, 157–64; Friel, 2013; TNA E364/54, E m1r–F m 2v and G m 2r E364/59, G m 2r; Friel, 1993, p.17; TNA E101/43/6, mm 1–6; E364/59 I, m 2v; TNA E364/61, J m 1r; TNA E364/59, I m 1r; Rose, 1982, pp.195, 198, 215 (the account on pp.211–16 is misdated to c. 1417; for the purchase of the flails see TNA E364/61, J m 1r); Crumlin-Pedersen, 2010, p.94; Hoheisel, 2009, pp.80–2; Johansen, 2009; McGrail, 2014, p.158; Hutchinson, 1997, pp.61–4; Ward, 2009, pp.162–7; Friel, 1993, pp.7–9; Friel, 1995, pp.157–64; TNA E101/185/7.

69   Friel, 1995, pp.169–80; Hutchinson, 1997, pp.36–41; TNA E364/54 D m 2v.

70   Ward, 2009, pp.167–70; Friel, 1995, pp.12–27; TNA E364/59, G m 2r.

71   Ward, 2009, pp.168–9.

72   TNA E364/54, G m 1r.

73   Anderson, 1926, pp.29, 48; Morrison, 1980.

74   Balard and Picard, 2014, pp.120–4; van der Merwe, 1983.

75   van der Merwe, 1981, pp.125–6; Bolton, 1980, p.152; Burwash, 1969, p.134.

76   Friel, 1994.

77   De Meer, n.d.

78   CCR 1409–13, pp.10–11, 35, 89; TNA E1010/44/17, mm 2, and 9r, 9v; CPR 1409–13, pp.13, 175, 178, 182, 310 and 321; TNA E364/61, L m 2v.

79   Friel, 1995, pp.55–6, 135; Crumlin-Pedersen, 2010, pp.55–6, 120–4; CCR 1413–19, p.19; TNA E364/59, G m 2v.

80 Burwash, 1969, pp.101–44.

81 Notes on balinger and barges: Burwash, 1969, pp.103–8; Friel, 1995, pp.146–50; Sayers, 2007; Sherborne, 1977; TNA E364/61, H m 2v and L m 1v; Rose, 1982, pp.42–3; TNA E364/54, E364/59 and E364/61 *passim*; TNA E403/637, mm 13–14; Friel, 2013; TNA E364/59, G m 2r; Alertz, 1995; Casson, 1995 and Bondioli, Burlet and Zysberg, 1995; TNA E101/44/17, m 11v.

82 Hutchinson, 1997, pp.150–3; Anderson, 1976, pp.42–51.

83 Images of castles: for example, Ewe 1972, pp.120, 128: ship on the seal of Dunwich, *c.* 1199; great seal of Danzig/Gdansk, 1400; Friel, 1995, pp.79–81.

84 TNA E364/61, J m2r and L m 1v.

85 TNA E364/54 G m 1v; E364/59, G m 2r; Taylor and Roskell, 1975, pp.165–7.

86 Mortimer, 2010, pp.216–18; Hildred, 2011, pp.579–86; Hardy, 2011.

87 TNA E364/61, K m2v.

88 Friel, 1995, pp.150–6; TNA E364/59, H m 1v, J m 2r and K m 2r; Hildred, 2011, pp.130–285, 307–512; CPR 1416–22, p.134; TNA E364/61, K m 1v.

89 TNA E364/54, E364/59 and E364/61, *passim*.

90 Sources: Rose, 2013, pp.115–39; Gardiner, 1976, nos 45 a–d; Gairdner, 1983, Vol. 3, pp.129–31; Guilmartin, 1974, pp 86–8; Rose, 2002, pp.84–5, 113–15.

91 Corbett, 1905, pp.15–24.

92 Rodger 2011.

93 Corbett, 1905, pp.1–14.

94 Cornwall Record Office AR/22/5, via http://discovery.nationalarchives.gov.uk

95 Taylor and Roskell, 1975, pp.162–7; McHardy, 2013.

96 CIM 1399–1422, nos 553–4, pp.313–17; Burwash, 1969, pp.125–7.

97 Nicolas, 1847, p.402; Allmand, 1992, pp.220–21; Rodger, 1997, p.143.

98 E101/44/23; E403/612, mm 2–3.

99 Information on the acquisition and service dates of most of the 1413–16 royal ships is in E364/54 D mm 2r–2v.

100 E364/54, F m 2v.

101 Allmand, 1992, pp.329–32; Pitcaithly, 2012, p.125; Marsden, 1915, pp.116–17.

102 CCR 1413–19, pp.94–5.

103 TNA E403/612, m 9.

104 E364/54 E m 2v and F m 1r.

105 Allmand, 1992, pp.67–73; Mortimer, 2010, pp.38–42, 105–6.

106 E364/54 D, m 2r and E364/61, I mm 1v–2v.

107 Mortimer, 2010, *loc. cit.*

108 TNA E364/54, E m 1r–F m 2v.

109 Richmond, 1971, pp.98–9, 112–18; Rodger, 1997, pp.145–7.

110 TNA E364/54, E m 1r–F m 2v; E364/61, I mm 1v–2v; CCR 1413–19, p.280; CPR 1413–16, pp.293–4; Allmand, 1992, p.69.

111   Nicolas, 1847, pp.406–7.
112   Mortimer, 2010, pp.154–5; Allmand, 1992, p.67; Rose, 2013, pp.160–2.
113   Invasion preparations: CCR 1413–19, pp.162, 176, 214; Mortimer, 2010, pp.105–6, 139–40; CPR 1413–16, p.294; TNA E364/54, E m 2v, F m 2r, G m 1r; RF9, pp.216–38; Wylie, 1914, p.449; Wylie, 1919, p.1.
114   Taylor and Roskell, 1975, pp.21–5; Hoskins and Curry, 2014, pp.37–40; tidal data for 14 August 1415 kindly supplied by UKHO (the UKHO data used in this book has been adjusted to take account of the differences between the medieval Julian Calendar and the modern Gregorian Calendar dates); Wylie, 1919, pp.17, 19–20; Taylor and Roskell, 1975, *loc. cit.*
115   Taylor and Roskell, 1975, pp.26–7.
116   Imray Chart no. 2110.7, 2014.
117   Taylor and Roskell, 1975, pp.30–1; Mortimer, 2010, pp.360–1, 369, 379–83; Allmand, 1992, pp.84–5; CPR 1413–16, pp.370, 382; TNA E403/623, m 4.
118   Wylie, 1919, pp.51, 95–6; De la Roncière, 1900, pp.212–13 n. 4.
119   TNA E364/54, E m 1r–F m 2; Wylie, 1919, pp.253–4.
120   TNA E364/54, E m 1r–F m 2.
121   TNA E403/623 mm 1–2.
122   Curry, 2007.
123   TNA E364/54, Dm2v–Fm1v.
124   TNA E403/623, mm 9–10; E364/54, D m 2v and F mm 1v–2v; E403/624 m 1 (1416); E364/59, J m 1r; Rose, 1982, pp.221–2.
125   Curry, 2007, pp.32–3; Wylie, 1919, pp.345, 347–8.
126   Given-Wilson et al., 2005, 'Henry V: March 1416', 49.XXV and XXVI; Given-Wilson et al., 2005, 'Henry V: October 1416', 26.V.
127   Taylor and Roskell, 1975, pp.134–5; De la Roncière, 1900, pp.216–17; CCR 1413–19, p.301.
128   TNA E403/623, m 14; CCR 1413–19, pp.303, 346; CPR 1416–22, p.70.
129   Wylie, 1919, pp.349–52; RF 9, pp.348–9; De la Roncière, 1900, pp.218–19; CPR 1416–22; Taylor and Roskell, 1975, pp.134–7, 140–3.
130   Allmand, 1992, pp.105–7; Rose, 1982, pp.281–321; TNA E403/624, mm 1–2; CPR 1416–22, pp.72–3; RF 9, pp.345–6, 350–1, 355–6; CCR 1413–19, p.303.
131   Wylie, 1919, pp.354–8; TNA E403/624, mm 3–4, 6–10, 15; Taylor and Roskell, 1975, pp.144–5.
132   Taylor and Roskell, 1975, *loc. cit.* and p.144 n. 1; Channel Pilot, 1996, p.35.
133   The following charts of the Seine Estuary were consulted online: Royal Museums Greenwich: PBD8264(5) Wagenhaer, *The Mariners Mirrour*, 1588 and G223: 1/1 Robert Dudley, *Carta quinta generale di Europa*, 1646 via http://collections.rmg.co.uk; via gallica.bnf.fr Bibliothèque Nationale de France,

Département Cartes et Plans: GE C-5088 (RES); Giacomo Giraldo of Venice, 1422; CPL GE C-5096 (RES), Piero Roselli, 1466; CPL GE D-7894 (RES), 16th century; MS 550, 1510 Dijon Portolan; GE C-5097 (RES) Gaspar Luis Vegas, 1534; *La Carte Générale du pays de Norma[n]die* ([Reprod. phot.]), M. Jan Jolivet, père, 1545 GE D-8476 (1897,390-391); Ge D 7897 Rés, Maggiolo, Giacomo 1560 (fragment); *Generale de Toutes les Cotes de France*, Sebastien Carmoisy, – 17th cent, ark:/12148/btv1b77100033, parts 4 and 5.

134 TNA E364/59, J m 1r.

135 Taylor and Roskell, 1975, pp.146–51; Barre, 1825, pp.6–9; Nicholas, 1847, pp.417–25; De la Roncière, 1900, pp.219–23; Morosini, 1899, pp.102–15; Bellaguet, 1844, pp.34–43; Wiltshire and Swindon History Centre, Earl of Radnor MS 490/1547.

136 Stevenson, 1861, pp.421–2; Curry, 2000, pp.435, 449–50; the original document is British Library Add MS 4603, no. 100.

137 E364/59, J m2r.

138 Curry, 2007, pp.40–1.

139 CCR 1413–19, p.317; Taylor and Roskell, 1975, pp.156–7.

140 CPR 1416–22, p.82; TNA E364/59, G m 2r; Taylor and Roskell, 1975, pp.156–7.

141 TNA E364/57; Given-Wilson et al., 2005, 'Henry V: October 1416'.

142 Given-Wilson et al., 2005, 'Henry V: October 1416', p.3.

143 TNA E101/48/12 and E101/48/13.

144 The 1417 seakeeping voyage: TNA E403/628, mm 8–11; Allmand, 1992, pp.228–9; CPR 1416–22, pp.74, 84–5; Nicholas, 1847, pp.429–30; E364/59, H mm 1r–2r; Wylie and Waugh, 1929, p.45.

145 TNA E403/628, mm 11–12.

146 Rodger, 1997, p.456; CCR 1413–19, 336, 339, 343, 391; Wylie and Waugh 1929, pp.36–49.

147 De la Roncière, 1900, p.226; TNA E364/59, G m 2r and I m 1v.

148 Wylie and Waugh, 1929, *loc. cit.*; De la Roncière, 1900, p.226; CPR 1416–22, pp.75, 136.

149 De la Roncière, 1900, p.226; E101/49/10 and E101/49/16.

150 TNA E101/49/10 and E101/49/16; E364/59, *passim*; CPR 1416–22, p.75; E101/48/26, m 1.

151 TNA E101/49/10 and E101/49/16 and Royal Museums Greenwich G223:1/1 via www.rmg.co.uk; Morosini, 1899, pp.134–41; Bellaguet, 1844, pp.96–101; De la Roncière, 1900, pp.226–9; Nicholas, 1847, pp.431–5; CPR 1416–22, p.142; Given-Wilson et al., 2005, 'Henry VI: October 1423', p.34

152 CPR 1416–22, pp.120–1.

153 Curry, 1994, p.45; TNA E364/57, I m 1r.

154 Allmand, 1992, pp.113–27.

155 TNA E101/49/10 and E101/49/16; Hardy, 1835, pp.320–29; CCR 1413–19, p.438.

156 CPR 1416–22, pp.144, 145; TNA E403/635, m 10; E403/635, m 11.

157 Allmand, 1992, p.229; TNA E403/635, mm 14 and 19; CPR 1416–122, pp.148, 196, 199.

158 CPR 1416–22, pp. 199–200; TNA E403/637, m 4.

159 CPR 1416–22, pp. 169, Rose 1982, p. 247.

160 CCR 1413–19, pp. 472–3, 505–6; TNA E403/637, mm 10–11; CPR 1416–22, p.202; Allmand, 1992, p.122.

161 Allmand, 1992, pp.122–7; Wylie and Waugh, 1929, pp.118–42; TNA E403/637, mm 13–14; E101/49/10 and E101/49/16; E101/49/27; E364/61 G m 1v and I m 2r.

162 CPR 1416–22, p.204.

163 Notes for this section: Chun, 2014, pp.70–81, 96–101; Holland, 1971, p.77; Platt, 1973, pp.107–18; Hughes, 1994; Kenyon, 1994; Rodger, 1997, p.115; TNA E403/637, mm 10–11; CCR 1413–19, p.525 and CPR 1416–22, p.209; RF 9, pp.792–3; Osborne, 2011, pp.42–57; TNA E364/59, H m 1r; TNA E101/49/29, mm 1 and 2; Rose, 1982, p.188.

164 TNA E364/59, M m 1r; E403/641, m 5; CCR 1413–19, p.27; CPR 1416–22, pp.209, 267; Rodger, 1997, pp.144–45, 456; Allmand, 1992, pp.228–9; RF 9, pp.792–3; Wylie and Waugh, 1929, pp.181–3, 197.

165 E364/59 and E364/61, *passim*.

166 Rose, 1977; the actual document is TNA E101/49/33, and includes information on the *Jesus* which is absent from the transcript.

167 TNA E403/645, mm 1–2.

168 Mortimer, 2010, p.288; Curry 2008; muster rolls of the Earl and Devon and Lord Botreaux: TNA E101/49/34; Trewarrak/Trevarrak information from www.medievalsoldier.org

169 Allmand, 1992, pp.128–50; Given-Wilson *et al.*, 2005, 'Henry V: December 1420', introduction, VI.17, XI.22 and XIII.23; Given-Wilson et al., 2005, 'Henry V: May 1421', Introduction, 22 and Appendix 7.

170 CPR 1416–22, p.329; E101/49/10, E101/49/16 and E403/646, m 16.

171 CPR 1416–22, p.324; CCR 1419–22, pp.170–1.

172 TNA E1010/49/10, and E101/49/16.

173 Allmand, 1992, pp.174–6; RF 10, p.256.

174 Rose, 1982, pp.52, 108–11, 113–14.

175 Prynne, 1977; Rose, 1982, pp.15–16; Friel, 1993, p.17.

176 1427–42: TNA E364/69, S m 2r; Friel, 1993, pp.10–11; E364/71, C mm 1r–2r; E101/53/5, ff 2v, 4v–7r, 34r E364/73, N mm 1r–1v; Rose, 1982, pp.235–36; E364/76, C mm 1r–1v.

177   TNA E364/81, G mm 1r–1v; E364/86, G mm 1r–1v.

178   Sobecki, 2008, pp.145–60; Wright, 1861, pp.159, 199; Gairdner, 1983, Vol. 3 pp.129–31.

179   Anderson, 1934; Prynne, 1968 and 1977; Friel, 1993, pp.11–18; Plets et al., 2009.

180   English Heritage, www.pastscape.org.uk/hob.aspx?hob_id=1082121.

181   TNA E364/54, E364/59, E364/61, Rose, 1982, CCR 1413–22 and CPR 1413–22, *passim*: other sources for specific pieces of information are indicated in each entry.

182   CPR 1416–22, p.387.

183   TNA E364/54, E364/59, E364/61, Rose, 1982, CCR 1413–22 and CPR 1413–22, *passim*: other sources for specific pieces of information are indicated in each entry.

184   Friel, 1993.

185   TNA E403/612, m 2.

186   Variant tonnage figures: E364/54, E m 1r; E364/59, M m 2r; rebuilding and disposal: Rose 1982, pp.65–6, 72–7.

187   TNA E364/59, J m 1r: the date of the sinking was not 22 May 1416 as in Rose, 1982, p.250.

188   TNA E364/54, D m 2v; CPR 1416–22, pp.71, 267; E403/637, m 13.

189   Rose, 1982, p.81.

190   CPR 1416–22, p.142.

191   CPR 1416–22, p.36.

192   TNA E403/628, m 16.

193   TNA E403/628, m 10.

194   TNA CPR 1416–22, p.142.

195   CPR 1416–22, pp.82, 267; TNA E403/637, mm 10–11 and 13–14.

196   CPR 1413–16, p.412.

197   E403/623 m 10.

198   CPR 1413–16, p.36; E403/612, m 2.

199   TNA E101/49/q0 and E101/49/16; Wylie and Waugh, 1929, p.318.

200   CPR 1413–16, p.412; TNA E403/637, m 4; E403/641, m 1.

201   CPR 1416–22, p.387.

202   CPR 1416–22, p.82; Ellis, 1827 pp.67–72.

203   Source for table: TNA E364/54, D m 2v–F m 2v.

INDEX

If you enjoyed this book, you may also be interested in…

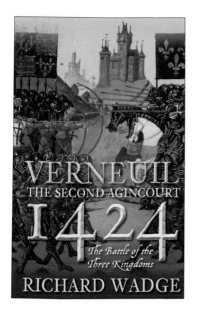

VERNEUIL 1424

The Second Agincourt – The Battle of the Three Kingdoms

RICHARD WADGE

9780750961134

In August 1424, the armies of England, Scotland and France met in the open fields outside the walls of Verneuil in a battle that would decide the future of the English conquests in France. The hero king, Henry V had been dead for two years and the French felt that this was their chance to avenge their startling defeat at Agincourt, and recover the lands that Henry had won from them. Despite its importance, the battle of Verneuil is largely overlooked in accounts of the Hundred Years War, and this book is the first proper account of the battle and its significance. It is also one of the first books to outline the important part the Scots played in the wars in France in the years between the two great battles of Agincourt and Verneuil.

᠂d discover thousands of
⌐oks.

᠁ss.co.uk